PANTRY STUFFERS

SOUP MIXES
Using Dehydrated Products

Wanda Bailey Clark

FURROW
PRESS

Edited by Edie Mourey www.furrowpress.com

Cover and interior design by David G. Danglis / Pinwheel Creative

Front cover photo: www.istockphoto.com / vusta.
Back cover photos: www.istockphoto.com / LauriPatterson; ganzoben; lucop
Interior icons: www.istockphoto.com / sv_sunny; browndogstudios

Printed in the United States of America
Library of Congress Control Number: 2012945163
International Standard Book Number: 978-0-9837561-5-6

Dedication

Every part of this cookbook is dedicated first to Jesus Christ, my Lord and Savior. I pray that this honors Him.

So many people have tasted recipes, provided feedback, and given encouragement, and—without their help—these recipes would have never been printed! Thank you from the bottom of my heart.

I give honor and appreciation to my husband, Paul, and to my family, who have willingly sacrificed their time with me.

To my beloved friend and business partner, Steve, and the beautiful love of his life, Jen, thank you for sharing the responsibility in bringing God's vision to reality.

Table of Recipes

Table of Recipes, cont'd.

Prepare Yourself

I am a suburban wife, mother, and grandmother. I have a great job that keeps me busy <u>more</u> than forty hours most weeks. Indeed, you could say I live a very full life—one where I'm not searching for more to do.

Many years ago, my mother-in-law instilled in me as a new bride the Proverbs 31 skills and wisdom to preserve all of the vegetables we would need for the year from "nature's bounty." Putting that wisdom into practice, kept her family well-fed through the Great Depression. Years before it became the subject of media attention, she passed on to me the suspicion of any preservative that is difficult to pronounce or not readily available in the grocery store.

My husband and I work very hard to preserve our own vegetables and fruits from our garden and local farmers markets. Because it was so much faster, we chose to freeze our fruits and vegetables instead of canning. However, when Hurricane Fran hit in September of 1996, the vulnerability of that strategy was clearly revealed. With Hurricane Fran, the power outages were widespread and affected <u>all</u> of the neighborhoods and businesses in our area. We had a generator, but ran out of gas after the first day only to find that we couldn't buy more. The gas stations were without power as well. We lost the year's worth of food we had stored in our three freezers. Fortunately, none of it was wasted. We would open the freezers once a day and pull out the food that had defrosted. We set up the grills and sent the kids out to knock on doors and invite neighbors to come and eat with us. During that time, we met and established friendships with neighbors that we cherish to this day.

Because canned vegetables do not require electricity, we decided to preserve as much as we could through canning. We also started to add relishes, jellies, and jams to our canned collection. We have a small home, and this new strategy revealed some additional challenges. Filled jars are heavy and take up a lot of room. And, like frozen vegetables, the shelf life is limited, which means all stored items must be dated and rotated to ensure that the oldest is always consumed first. It is painful to throw away fruits of your hard labor when you don't manage expirations effectively.

In 2010, the economic woes took on a new reality for me when the company I had been working for more than fourteen years filed bankruptcy and was ordered by the courts to be divided and sold. The severance, retirement, and stock options that were a major part of my well-planned financial future all disappeared. That opened my eyes to see how similar the United States economy resembled the times just before the Great Depression that my mother-in-law had shared with me. As Proverbs 27:12 says, "A sensible person sees danger and takes cover; the inexperienced keep going and are punished."

What I needed was a way to be more prepared with less space, less weight, and a longer shelf life. My research led me to dehydrated food products and ready-to-eat prepackaged meal packets. My finances were limited, but I felt the easiest way to go was to purchase prepackaged meals. Unless you can afford to purchase in volume, they are very expensive. I ordered several trial samples. My family didn't like them.

Next, I ordered a variety of dehydrated vegetables. I was impressed by how light-weight they were—but was not prepared for their appearance. They looked more like confetti than vegetables. But, learning the nutritional value encouraged me. Learning that the nutritional value degraded after a couple of months unless they were repack-aged away from light and air steered me toward packaging my own mixes.

I tried cooking the dehydrated vegetables the same way I would canned or frozen vegetables. The results were not good. It took me a lot of time, research, and experimen-tation to get results that my family liked and that could be stored to keep the nutritional values at their peak. Convenience is a priority for me. But controlling chemical additives in my family's foods is equally important.

As I was going through my extensive collection of recipes to convert and test, I found myself thinking about how many additional ingredients I would have to keep on hand and available to add to the mixes before cooking. On a whim, I started to search for additional dehydrated products. That's when an exciting adventure began. I discov-ered a whole world of dehydrated products that I never knew existed! I discovered that dehydrated or freeze-dried butter, eggs, wine, cheese, soy sauce, teriyaki sauce, sour cream, cream cheese, peanut butter, and many other products were available for purchase.

Having access to so many dehydrated products gave me the flexibility to create recipes, many that can be prepared adding only water. In addition to our personal stor-age needs, limiting the added ingredients made the recipes a good fit when we went camping or boating.

The next hurdle to overcome was serving size. A number of the recipes I converted to work with the dehydrated products yielded eight or more servings. That was simply too much for us, and I could not deal with the waste of throwing away so many left-overs. I surveyed family and friends and determined that most families would be best served if there were packaging options to support small, medium, and large servings. Recipes using dehydrated ingredients can be scaled to support any serving size.

God gave me a vision to create this cookbook, and other cookbooks to follow—to share with others the knowledge and skills I have acquired through my experiences and discoveries. My mother-in-law passed on to me the knowledge and skills that were hers because of what her mother taught her. She combined that with what she discovered through her own experiences. My generation has been spoiled with convenience and has failed the biblical charge to learn and pass down the skills and wisdom to the next generation.

My nature would be to take care of everyone! But, as the old Chinese proverb says, "Give a man a fish and he will eat for a day, teach a man to fish and he will eat for a lifetime."

Dehydrated food products add convenience and survival storage options that are affordable, lightweight, and have a long shelf life. The goal of this book is to teach those willing to learn how to create soup mixes using dehydrated products. Those who choose to learn will be better equipped with additional knowledge and skills to better survive whatever storms life brings their way.

I am excited about this cookbook. I view it—and the other cookbooks to follow— as an exciting new adventure!!

— Wanda Bailey Clark

The Basics

In the recipes that soon follow, you will notice that dehydrated foods are not the only non-perishable products used. All of the primary ingredients listed in the recipes are dehydrated, freeze-dried, or powdered.

Dehydration/Freeze-Drying Process

Dehydration is the oldest, most natural form of food preservation. Ancient civilizations used various forms of open-air drying to dry vegetables and fruits to preserve food for future use. Modern dehydrators use controlled air and heat to effectively remove the moisture content from vegetables and fruits.

Freeze-drying is dehydration that works by freezing and then reducing the pressure to allow the frozen water in the material to sublimate directly from the solid phase to the gas phase.

Nutritional Value

Most vitamins and minerals remain intact during the dehydration process, except for vitamin C which does not tolerate the dehydration process. Dehydration retains more vitamin and mineral content than canned or frozen vegetables. It has also been suggested by many that, in some cases, if the fresh produce in the grocery store has been picked while green and has traveled for days before arriving at the store, then dehydrated vegetables even have a higher vitamin and mineral content than their fresh counterparts.

Setting Expectations

Like all food preservation methods, dehydration does alter taste. If you have never cooked with dehydrated vegetables, I recommend trying the following experiment.

Cook one pot of fresh green beans, one pot of canned green beans, and one pot of frozen green beans, seasoning them all exactly the same way. Taste a sample from each pot. You will notice that each tastes like green beans. However, each sample has a slightly different taste.

Dehydrated green beans that have been rehydrated and cooked will also taste like green beans. In appearance, however, they more closely resemble canned green beens.

One thing to keep in mind is that dehydration intensifies the flavor of some vegetables while it lessens the flavor intensity of others.

Using the Recipes

The purpose of this cookbook is to provide a variety of soup mixes that will appeal to a wide range of tastes. The mixes may be prepared and packaged for storage. Or if you have dehydrated products in your pantry, you may use these recipes like those in a traditional cookbook.

TVP Products

You will notice Textured Vegetable Protein (TVP) products in many of the recipes. The TVP products are high in protein and have the flavor and texture of beef, chicken, and ham, respectively. Although these products have the flavor of meat, there is no meat in them, and they are considered vegan.

You may use dehydrated beef, chicken, or ham instead of the TVP products in the mixes; or you may exclude the TVP products from your recipe packets and add meat before cooking your soup. Dehydrated meats significantly increase the cost per serving of the soup mixes. For example, a TVP product typically costs thirty cents per ounce while the dehydrated meat product will cost two dollars per ounce.

Storing the Soup Mixes

Special care should be used to keep dehydrated vegetables away from all light and moisture. The shelf life of dehydrated vegetable soup mixes is extended or shortened by the storage method and storage conditions. Heat and humidity can reduce the shelf life.

Mixes stored in freezer bags will typically last six to eight months in the pantry, but longer if stored in the freezer. Mixes stored in mason jars will typically last up to two years. Mixes stored in vacuum heat-sealed bags will typically last a minimum of eight years. Most experts estimate the shelf life of well packaged dehydrated food products to be twenty-five years.

HELPFUL TIP: Before creating any mixes for storage, prepare and cook a 1-2 serving size of the mix. Make any needed adjustments to the seasonings to suit your tastes.

HELPFUL TIP: Some dehydrated products, such as powdered tomato and powdered eggs, are subject to clumping. This does not affect the usability of the products, but the clumping may be lessened by storing a silicon packet in the food mix.

The Icons

Icons denote information about ingredients and preparation.

 Indicates that the recipe is fully vegan, containing no meat, dairy, or egg byproducts.

 Indicates that the recipe includes seasonings that contain beef byproducts or beef additions.

 Indicates that the recipe includes seasonings that contain poultry byproducts or poultry additions.

 Indicates that the recipe includes seasonings that contain pork byproducts or pork additions.

 Indicates that the recipe includes seasonings that contain seafood byproducts or seafood additions.

 Indicates that the recipe contains dairy or dairy byproducts.

 Indicates that the recipe contains egg or egg byproducts.

 Indicates that the recipe contains wheat or wheat byproducts.

 Indicates that the recipe contains fruit or fruit byproducts.

 Indicates that the recipe contains nuts or nut byproducts.

 Indicates that the recipe gives the option to blend or cream all or part of the recipe contents.

How to Read the Recipes

Celery Soup

Icons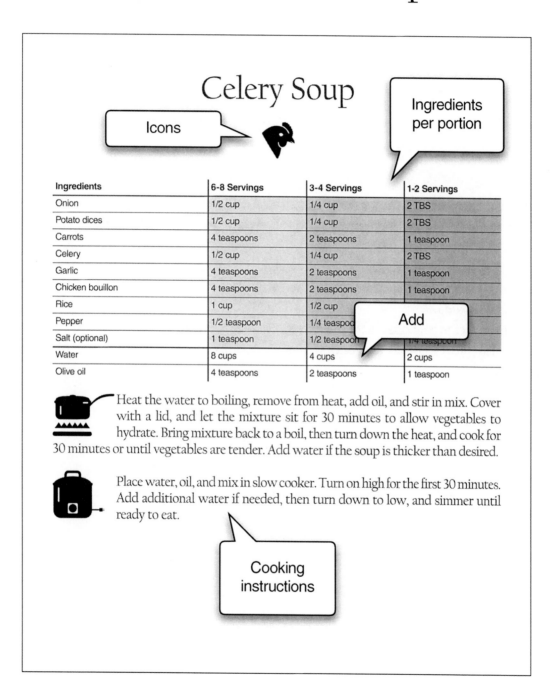

Ingredients per portion

Ingredients	6-8 Servings	3-4 Servings	1-2 Servings
Onion	1/2 cup	1/4 cup	2 TBS
Potato dices	1/2 cup	1/4 cup	2 TBS
Carrots	4 teaspoons	2 teaspoons	1 teaspoon
Celery	1/2 cup	1/4 cup	2 TBS
Garlic	4 teaspoons	2 teaspoons	1 teaspoon
Chicken bouillon	4 teaspoons	2 teaspoons	1 teaspoon
Rice	1 cup	1/2 cup	
Pepper	1/2 teaspoon	1/4 teaspoon	
Salt (optional)	1 teaspoon	1/2 teaspoon	1/4 teaspoon
Water	8 cups	4 cups	2 cups
Olive oil	4 teaspoons	2 teaspoons	1 teaspoon

Add

Heat the water to boiling, remove from heat, add oil, and stir in mix. Cover with a lid, and let the mixture sit for 30 minutes to allow vegetables to hydrate. Bring mixture back to a boil, then turn down the heat, and cook for 30 minutes or until vegetables are tender. Add water if the soup is thicker than desired.

Place water, oil, and mix in slow cooker. Turn on high for the first 30 minutes. Add additional water if needed, then turn down to low, and simmer until ready to eat.

Cooking instructions

Ingredients per Portion

Each recipe has been scaled for three different serving sizes—1-2 servings, 3-4 servings, and 6-8 servings. The soup mix ingredients are listed by these portion sizes. All of the ingredients that can be packaged in a mix are listed above the bold line. All ingredients that must be added to a mix are below the bold line.

SPECIAL TIP: All ingredients above the bold line are dehydrated, freeze-dried, or powdered ingredients. However, you don't have to include all of the ingredients in a packet. You may move any ingredients down to the non-dehydrated line if you choose.

Cooking Instructions

The cooking instructions for every dehydrated soup mix consist of two parts—rehydrating the dehydrated ingredients and cooking the ingredients. Rehydrated ingredients cook much faster than fresh.

Mixes can be rehydrated with cold water, but rehydrate faster in hot water. Each stove top recipe recommends that the mix be allowed to sit in hot water for 30 minutes prior to cooking.

Each recipe contains cooking instructions for both stove top and slow cooker. You may also find variations that offer the use of one non-perishable product in place of another.

SPECIAL TIP: It is best if you put a lid on the pot while the soups rehydrate and cook with no lid, stirring often.

SPECIAL TIP: You may choose to cook the mix continually without allowing the mix to rehydrate as it cooks. In this case, you will need to add additional water as the mix cooks, stirring it often during the entire cooking process.

Vegetable Soup Mixes

Vegetable-Based Soups

This section includes a collection of soups made with various dehydrated vegetables. The shriveled state of dehydrated vegetables may make them seem less appetizing at first glance, but the taste and nutritional value are pleasantly surprising.

BELL PEPPER: Good source of vitamin E and contains more than 30 different carotenoids, including excellent amounts of beta-carotene and zeaxanthin.

BROCCOLI: Good source of protein, thiamin, niacin, pantothenic acid, calcium, iron and selenium, and a very good source of vitamin A, vitamin C, riboflavin, vitamin B6, folate, magnesium, phosphorus, potassium, and manganese.

CABBAGE: Good source of vitamin A, thiamin, vitamin B6, calcium, iron and magnesium, and a very good source of dietary fiber, vitamin C, folate, potassium, and manganese.

CARROT: Root vegetable with health benefiting compounds such as beta-carotenes, vitamin A, minerals, and anti-oxidants in ample amounts.

CELERY: Contains vitamin C and active compounds that promote health, including phthalides, which may help lower cholesterol, and coumarins, that may be useful in cancer prevention.

CORN: Good source of vitamin C and folate.

GREEN BEANS: Good source of thiamin, riboflavin, calcium, iron, magnesium, phosphorus, and potassium. Alsoa very good source of dietary fiber, vitamin A, vitamin C, vitamin K, and manganese.

MUSHROOM: An excellent source of antioxidants (considered a fungus).

ONION: Good source of dietary fiber, folate, potassium, and manganese. A very good source of vitamin C and vitamin B6.

POTATO: High fiber food that offers significant protection against cardiovascular disease and cancer. Good source of vitamin B6, vitamin C, copper, potassium, manganese, and dietary fiber. Good source of anti-oxidants, which exhibit activity against free radicals.

SPINACH: Good source of protein, phosphorus, and zinc. A very good source of dietary fiber, vitamin A, vitamin C, vitamin E (alpha-Tocopherol), vitamin K, thiamin, riboflavin, vitamin B6, folate, calcium, iron, magnesium, potassium, copper, manganese, and selenium.

TOMATO: Good source of dietary fiber, thiamin, riboflavin, vitamin B6, iron, magnesium, and phosphorus. A very good source of vitamin C, niacin, folate, potassium, copper, and manganese.

Cheesy Vegetable Soup

Ingredients	6-8 Servings	3-4 Servings	1-2 Servings
Potato dices	1 cup	1/2 cup	1/4 cup
Celery	4 teaspoons	2 teaspoons	1 teaspoon
Carrots	4 teaspoons	2 teaspoons	1 teaspoon
Mixed peppers	1 teaspoon	1/2 teaspoon	1/4 teaspoon
Dry milk	1/3 cup	8 teaspoons	4 teaspoons
All purpose flour	4 teaspoons	2 teaspoons	1 teaspoon
Instant potato flakes	1/2 cup	1/4 cup	2 TBS
Cheddar cheese powder	1/2 cup	1/4 cup	2 TBS
Chicken bouillon	4 teaspoons	2 teaspoons	1 teaspoon
Nutmeg	1/4 teaspoon	1/8 teaspoon	1/16 teaspoon
Pepper	1/2 teaspoon	1/4 teaspoon	1/8 teaspoon
Salt (optional)	1/2 teaspoon	1/4 teaspoon	1/8 teaspoon
Water	8 cups	4 cups	2 cups

Heat the water to boiling, remove from heat, and stir in mix. Cover with a lid, and let the mixture sit for 30 minutes to allow vegetables to hydrate. Bring mixture back to a boil, then turn down the heat, and cook for 30 minutes or until vegetables are tender. Add water if the soup is thicker than desired.

Place water and mix in slow cooker. Turn on high for the first 30 minutes. Add additional water if needed, then turn down to low, and simmer until ready to eat.

VARIATION: You may substitute potato starch for the potato flakes.

Oriental Vegetable Soup

Ingredients	6-8 Servings	3-4 Servings	1-2 Servings
Mushrooms	1 cup	1/2 cup	1/4 cup
Carrots	4 teaspoons	2 teaspoons	1 teaspoon
Onion	4 teaspoons	2 teaspoons	1 teaspoon
Leeks	4 teaspoons	2 teaspoons	1 teaspoon
Spinach	4 teaspoons	2 teaspoons	1 teaspoon
Broccoli	4 teaspoons	2 teaspoons	1 teaspoon
Cabbage	4 teaspoons	2 teaspoons	1 teaspoon
Cayenne pepper	1/4 teaspoon	1/8 teaspoon	1/16 teaspoon
Ginger	2 teaspoons	1 teaspoon	1/2 teaspoon
Soy sauce powder	2 teaspoons	1 teaspoon	1/2 teaspoon
Teriyaki powder	2 teaspoons	1 teaspoon	1/2 teaspoon
Vinegar powder	4 teaspoons	2 teaspoons	1 teaspoon
Cloves	1/2 teaspoon	1/4 teaspoon	1/8 teaspoon
Garlic	1 teaspoon	1/2 teaspoon	1/4 teaspoon
Chicken bouillon	4 teaspoons	2 teaspoons	1 teaspoon
Chinese noodles	2/3 cup	1/3 cup	8 teaspoons
Pepper	1/2 teaspoon	1/4 teaspoon	1/8 teaspoon
Salt (optional)	1/2 teaspoon	1/4 teaspoon	1/8 teaspoon
Water	8 cups	4 cups	2 cups
Canola oil	4 teaspoons	2 teaspoons	1 teaspoon

Heat the water to boiling, remove from heat, add oil, and stir in mix. Cover with a lid, and let the mixture sit for 30 minutes to allow vegetables to hydrate. Bring mixture back to a boil, then turn down the heat, and cook for 30 minutes or until vegetables are tender. Add water if the soup is thicker than desired.

Place water, oil, and mix in slow cooker. Turn on high for the first 30 minutes. Add additional water if needed, then turn down to low, and simmer until ready to eat.

Garden Vegetable Soup

Ingredients	6-8 Servings	3-4 Servings	1-2 Servings
Leeks	4 teaspoons	2 teaspoons	1 teaspoon
Carrots	4 teaspoons	2 teaspoons	1 teaspoon
Potato dices	1 cup	1/2 cup	1/4 cup
Onion	1/4 cup	2 TBS	1 TBS
Green beans	4 teaspoons	2 teaspoons	1 teaspoon
Tomato dices	1/3 cup	3 TBS	4 teaspoons
Tomato powder	1/3 cup	3 TBS	4 teaspoons
Sugar	3 TBS	4 teaspoons	2 teaspoons
Corn	1/4 cup	2 TBS	1 TBS
Parsley	1/4 cup	2 TBS	1 TBS
Lemon juice powder	4 teaspoons	2 teaspoons	1 teaspoon
Chicken bouillon	4 teaspoons	2 teaspoons	1 teaspoon
Garlic	8 teaspoons	4 teaspoons	2 teaspoons
Pepper	1/2 teaspoon	1/4 teaspoon	1/8 teaspoon
Salt (optional)	1/2 teaspoon	1/4 teaspoon	1/8 teaspoon
Water	8 cups	4 cups	2 cups
Olive oil	4 teaspoons	2 teaspoons	1 teaspoon

 Heat the water to boiling, remove from heat, add oil, and stir in mix. Cover with a lid, and let the mixture sit for 30 minutes to allow vegetables to hydrate. Bring mixture back to a boil, then turn down the heat, and cook for 30 minutes or until vegetables are tender. Add water if the soup is thicker than desired.

Place water, oil, and mix in slow cooker. Turn on high for the first 30 minutes. Add additional water if needed, then turn down to low, and simmer until ready to eat.

Vegetable Pasta Soup

Ingredients	6-8 Servings	3-4 Servings	1-2 Servings
Spinach	1/4 cup	2 TBS	1 TBS
Zucchini	1/4 cup	2 TBS	1 TBS
Mushrooms	1 cup	1/2 cup	1/4 cup
Onion	1/4 cup	2 TBS	1 TBS
Mixed peppers	2 teaspoons	1 teaspoon	1/2 teaspoon
Basil	2 teaspoons	1 teaspoon	1/2 teaspoon
Garlic	4 teaspoons	2 teaspoons	1 teaspoon
Nutmeg	1/2 teaspoon	1/4 teaspoon	1/8 teaspoon
Butter powder	1/4 cup	2 TBS	1 TBS
All purpose flour	8 teaspoons	4 teaspoons	2 teaspoons
Dry milk	1/2 cup	1/4 cup	2 TBS
White cheese powder	1/2 cup	1/4 cup	2 TBS
Parmesan cheese	1/2 cup	1/4 cup	2 TBS
Sour cream powder	1/2 cup	1/4 cup	2 TBS
Pepper	1/2 teaspoon	1/4 teaspoon	1/8 teaspoon
Salt (optional)	1/2 teaspoon	1/4 teaspoon	1/8 teaspoon
Water	8 cups	4 cups	2 cups
Olive oil	4 teaspoons	2 teaspoons	1 teaspoon
Cooked curly pasta	4 cups	2 cups	1 cup

 Heat the water to boiling, remove from heat, add oil, and stir in mix. Cover with a lid, and let the mixture sit for 30 minutes to allow vegetables to hydrate. Bring mixture back to a boil, then turn down the heat, and cook for 30 minutes or until vegetables are tender. Add water if the soup is thicker than desired.

 Place water, oil, and mix in slow cooker. Turn on high for the first 30 minutes. Add additional water if needed, then turn down to low, and simmer until ready to eat.

Use conventional or stick blender to cream the mixture. Cook the mixture for 30 additional minutes. Mix over cooked and drained pasta. Top with parmesan cheese before serving.

Creamy Carrots and Pasta Soup

Ingredients	6-8 Servings	3-4 Servings	1-2 Servings
Chicken bouillon	4 teaspoons	2 teaspoons	1 teaspoon
Carrots	1/2 cup	1/4 cup	2 TBS
Potato dices	1 cup	1/2 cup	1/4 cup
Onion	1/4 cup	2 TBS	1 TBS
Ginger	1 teaspoon	1/2 teaspoon	1/4 teaspoon
Jamaican jerk seasoning	1 teaspoon	1/2 teaspoon	1/4 teaspoon
Dry milk	1/3 cup	8 teaspoons	4 teaspoons
Water	8 cups	4 cups	2 cups
Cooked pasta (like rotini)	4 cups	2 cups	1 cup

 Heat the water to boiling, remove from heat and stir in mix. Cover with a lid, and let the mixture sit for 30 minutes to allow vegetables to hydrate. Bring mixture back to a boil, then turn down the heat, and cook for 30 minutes or until vegetables are tender. Add water if the soup is thicker than desired.

 Place water and mix in slow cooker. Turn on high for the first 30 minutes. Add additional water if needed, then turn down to low, and simmer until ready to eat.

For a creamier soup, take 1/4 to 1/2 of mixture and blend in a traditional blender, blend with a stick blender, or mash with a potato masher and whip with a fork. Pour mixture over cooked and drained pasta.

Rich Tomato Soup

Ingredients	6-8 Servings	3-4 Servings	1-2 Servings
Onion	1/4 cup	2 TBS	1 TBS
Garlic	4 teaspoons	2 teaspoons	1 teaspoon
Basil	8 teaspoons	4 teaspoons	2 teaspoons
Tomato powder	1 cup	1/2 cup	1/4 cup
Tomato dices	2 cups	1 cup	1/2 cup
Sugar	4 teaspoons	2 teaspoons	1 teaspoon
Beef bouillon	4 teaspoons	2 teaspoons	1 teaspoon
Dry milk	1/4 cup	2 TBS	1 TBS
Pepper	2 teaspoons	1 teaspoon	1/2 teaspoon
Salt (optional)	2 teaspoons	1 teaspoon	1/2 teaspoon
Water	8 cups	4 cups	2 cups
Olive oil	4 teaspoons	2 teaspoons	1 teaspoon

Heat the water to boiling, remove from heat, and stir in mix. Cover with a lid, and let the mixture sit for 30 minutes to allow vegetables to hydrate. Bring mixture back to a boil, then turn down the heat, and cook for 30 minutes or until vegetables are tender. Add water if the soup is thicker than desired.

Place water and mix in slow cooker. Turn on high for the first 30 minutes. Add additional water if needed, then turn down to low, and simmer until ready to eat.

For a creamy consistency, use a traditional or stick blender and blend to a smooth consistency before serving.

VARIATION: You may substitute potato starch for the instant potato flakes.

Tomato and Spinach Soup

Ingredients	6-8 Servings	3-4 Servings	1-2 Servings
TVP ham bits	1 cup	1/2 cup	1/4 cup
Onion	1/2 cup	1/4 cup	2 TBS
Garlic	4 teaspoons	2 teaspoons	1 teaspoon
Tomato powder	2/3 cup	1/3 cup	8 teaspoons
Butter powder	1/2 cup	1/4 cup	2 TBS
Sugar	4 teaspoons	2 teaspoons	1 teaspoon
Tomato dices	2/3 cup	1/3 cup	8 teaspoons
Chicken bouillon	4 teaspoons	2 teaspoons	1 teaspoon
Spinach	2/3 cup	1/3 cup	8 teaspoons
Parmesan cheese	1/4 cup	2 TBS	1 TBS
Pepper	1 teaspoon	1/2 teaspoon	1/4 teaspoon
Nutmeg	1/2 teaspoon	1/4 teaspoon	1/8 teaspoon
Water	8 cups	4 cups	2 cups
Olive oil	4 teaspoons	2 teaspoons	1 teaspoon

Heat the water to boiling, remove from heat, add oil, and stir in mix. Cover with a lid, and let the mixture sit for 30 minutes to allow vegetables to hydrate. Bring mixture back to a boil, then turn down the heat, and cook for 30 minutes or until vegetables are tender. Add water if the soup is thicker than desired.

Place water, oil, and mix in slow cooker. Turn on high for the first 30 minutes. Add additional water if needed, then turn down to low, and simmer until ready to eat.

Celery Soup

Ingredients	6-8 Servings	3-4 Servings	1-2 Servings
Onion	1/2 cup	1/4 cup	2 TBS
Potato dices	1/2 cup	1/4 cup	2 TBS
Carrots	4 teaspoons	2 teaspoons	1 teaspoon
Celery	1/2 cup	1/4 cup	2 TBS
Garlic	4 teaspoons	2 teaspoons	1 teaspoon
Chicken bouillon	4 teaspoons	2 teaspoons	1 teaspoon
Rice	1 cup	1/2 cup	1/4 cup
Pepper	1/2 teaspoon	1/4 teaspoon	1/8 teaspoon
Salt (optional)	1 teaspoon	1/2 teaspoon	1/4 teaspoon
Water	8 cups	4 cups	2 cups
Olive oil	4 teaspoons	2 teaspoons	1 teaspoon

Heat the water to boiling, remove from heat, add oil, and stir in mix. Cover with a lid, and let the mixture sit for 30 minutes to allow vegetables to hydrate. Bring mixture back to a boil, then turn down the heat, and cook for 30 minutes or until vegetables are tender. Add water if the soup is thicker than desired.

Place water, oil, and mix in slow cooker. Turn on high for the first 30 minutes. Add additional water if needed, then turn down to low, and simmer until ready to eat.

TVP Ham Oriental Soup

Ingredients	6-8 Servings	3-4 Servings	1-2 Servings
Chicken bouillon	4 teaspoons	2 teaspoons	1 teaspoon
Onion	1/4 cup	2 TBS	1 TBS
Carrots	4 teaspoons	2 teaspoons	1 teaspoon
Cabbage	4 teaspoons	2 teaspoons	1 teaspoon
Spinach	8 teaspoons	4 teaspoons	2 teaspoons
Soy sauce powder	4 teaspoons	2 teaspoons	1 teaspoon
Red wine powder	1/4 cup	2 TBS	1 TBS
Garlic	4 teaspoons	2 teaspoons	1 teaspoon
TVP ham bits	1 cup	1/2 cup	1/4 cup
Egg noodles	1 cup	1/2 cup	1/4 cup
Pepper	1/2 teaspoon	1/4 teaspoon	1/8 teaspoon
Water	8 cups	4 cups	2 cups
Olive Oil	4 teaspoons	2 teaspoons	1 teaspoon

Heat the water to boiling, remove from heat, add oil, and stir in mix. Cover with a lid, and let the mixture sit for 30 minutes to allow vegetables to hydrate. Bring mixture back to a boil, then turn down the heat, and cook for 30 minutes or until vegetables are tender. Add water if the soup is thicker than desired.

Place water, oil, and mix in slow cooker. Turn on high for the first 30 minutes. Add additional water if needed, then turn down to low, and simmer until ready to eat.

Broccoli Cheese Soup

Ingredients	6-8 Servings	3-4 Servings	1-2 Servings
Onion	1/4 cup	2 TBS	1 TBS
Broccoli	1 cup	1/2 cup	1/4 cup
Cheddar cheese powder	1/2 cup	1/4 cup	2 TBS
Sour cream powder	4 teaspoons	2 teaspoons	1 teaspoon
Butter powder	4 teaspoons	2 teaspoons	1 teaspoon
All purpose flour	1/2 cup	1/4 cup	2 TBS
Parsley	4 teaspoons	2 teaspoons	1 teaspoon
Chicken bouillon	4 teaspoons	2 teaspoons	1 teaspoon
Dry milk	1 cup	1/2 cup	1/4 cup
Pepper	1/2 teaspoon	1/4 teaspoon	1/8 teaspoon
Salt (optional)	1 teaspoon	1/2 teaspoon	1/4 teaspoon
Water	8 cups	4 cups	2 cups
Canola oil	4 teaspoons	2 teaspoons	1 teaspoon

Heat the water to boiling, remove from heat, add oil, and stir in mix. Cover with a lid, and let the mixture sit for 30 minutes to allow vegetables to hydrate. Bring mixture back to a boil, then turn down the heat, and cook for 30 minutes or until vegetables are tender. Add water if the soup is thicker than desired.

Place water, oil, and mix in slow cooker. Turn on high for the first 30 minutes. Add additional water if needed, then turn down to low, and simmer until ready to eat.

Sour Cream Potato Soup

Ingredients	6-8 Servings	3-4 Servings	1-2 Servings
Potato dices	1 cup	1/2 cup	1/4 cup
Celery	2 teaspoons	1 teaspoon	1/2 teaspoon
Onion	1/4 cup	2 TBS	1 TBS
TVP ham bits	1/2 cup	1/4 cup	2 TBS
Chicken bouillon	4 teaspoons	2 teaspoons	1 teaspoon
Instant potato flakes	4 teaspoons	2 teaspoons	1 teaspoon
Dry milk	1/4 cup	2 TBS	1 TBS
Sour cream powder	1/2 cup	1/4 cup	2 TBS
Butter powder	8 teaspoons	4 teaspoons	2 teaspoons
Pepper	1/2 teaspoon	1/4 teaspoon	1/8 teaspoon
Salt	1/2 teaspoon	1/4 teaspoon	1/8 teaspoon
Water	8 cups	4 cups	2 cups
Canola oil	4 teaspoons	2 teaspoons	1 teaspoon

Heat the water to boiling, remove from heat, add oil, and stir in mix. Cover with a lid, and let the mixture sit for 30 minutes to allow vegetables to hydrate. Bring mixture back to a boil, then turn down the heat, and cook for 30 minutes or until vegetables are tender. Add water if the soup is thicker than desired.

Place water, oil, and mix in slow cooker. Turn on high for the first 30 minutes. Add additional water if needed, then turn down to low, and simmer until ready to eat.

Classic Potato Soup

Ingredients	6-8 Servings	3-4 Servings	1-2 Servings
Potato dices	1 cup	1/2 cup	1/4 cup
Celery	2 teaspoons	1 teaspoon	1/2 teaspoon
Onion	1/4 cup	2 TBS	1 TBS
Carrots	4 teaspoons	2 teaspoons	1 teaspoon
Garlic	1 teaspoon	1/2 teaspoon	1/4 teaspoon
Thyme	2 teaspoons	1 teaspoon	1/2 teaspoon
Chicken bouillon	2 teaspoons	1 teaspoon	1/2 teaspoon
Dry milk	2/3 cup	1/3 cup	8 teaspoons
Instant potato flakes	1/2 cup	1/4 cup	2 TBS
Butter powder	1/4 cup	2 TBS	1 TBS
Pepper	1/2 teaspoon	1/4 teaspoon	1/8 teaspoon
Salt	1/2 teaspoon	1/4 teaspoon	1/8 teaspoon
Water	8 cups	4 cups	2 cups

Heat the water to boiling, remove from heat, and stir in mix. Cover with a lid, and let the mixture sit for 30 minutes to allow vegetables to hydrate. Bring mixture back to a boil, then turn down the heat, and cook for 30 minutes or until vegetables are tender. Add water if the soup is thicker than desired.

Place water and mix in slow cooker. Turn on high for the first 30 minutes. Add additional water if needed, then turn down to low, and simmer until ready to eat.

Cheesy Potato Soup

Ingredients	6-8 Servings	3-4 Servings	1-2 Servings
Potato dices	2 cups	1 cup	1/2 cup
Onion	1/4 cup	2 TBS	1 TBS
TVP ham bits	1/2 cup	1/4 cup	2 TBS
Chives	4 teaspoons	2 teaspoons	1 teaspoon
Cheddar cheese powder	1/4 cup	2 TBS	1 TBS
Instant potato flakes	1/4 cup	2 TBS	1 TBS
Dry milk	2/3 cup	1/3 cup	3 TBS
Sour cream powder	1/4 cup	2 TBS	1 TBS
Butter powder	1/4 cup	2 TBS	1 TBS
Pepper	1/2 teaspoon	1/4 teaspoon	1/8 teaspoon
Salt	1/2 teaspoon	1/4 teaspoon	1/8 teaspoon
Water	8 cups	4 cups	2 cups

Heat the water to boiling, remove from heat, and stir in mix. Cover with a lid, and let the mixture sit for 30 minutes to allow vegetables to hydrate. Bring mixture back to a boil, then turn down the heat, and cook for 30 minutes or until vegetables are tender. Add water if the soup is thicker than desired.

Place water and mix in slow cooker. Turn on high for the first 30 minutes. Add additional water if needed, then turn down to low, and simmer until ready to eat.

TVP Ham Potato Soup

Ingredients	6-8 Servings	3-4 Servings	1-2 Servings
Potato dices	1 cup	1/2 cup	1/4 cup
Onion	8 teaspoons	4 teaspoons	2 teaspoons
Leeks	4 teaspoons	2 teaspoons	1 teaspoon
Butter powder	4 teaspoons	2 teaspoons	1 teaspoon
Thyme	2 teaspoons	1 teaspoon	1/2 teaspoon
Basil	2 teaspoons	1 teaspoon	1/2 teaspoon
Dry milk	1/4 cup	2 TBS	1 TBS
TVP ham bits	1 cup	1/2 cup	1/4 cup
Chicken bouillon	4 teaspoons	2 teaspoons	1 teaspoon
Instant potato flakes	1/2 cup	1/4 cup	2 TBS
Pepper	1/2 teaspoon	1/4 teaspoon	1/8 teaspoon
Salt (optional)	1/2 teaspoon	1/4 teaspoon	1/8 teaspoon
Water	8 cups	4 cups	2 cups

 Heat the water to boiling, remove from heat, add oil, and stir in mix. Cover with a lid, and let the mixture sit for 30 minutes to allow vegetables to hydrate. Bring mixture back to a boil, then turn down the heat and cook for 30 minutes or until vegetables tender. Add water if the soup is thicker than desired.

 Place water, oil, and mix in crock pot. Turn on high for the first 30 minutes. Add additional water if needed, then turn down to low and simmer until ready to eat.

Place water, oil, and mix in crock pot. Turn on high for the first 30 minutes. Add additional water if needed, then turn down to low and simmer until ready to eat.

Italian Style Soup Mixes

Italian Soup Mixes

The soup mixes in this section reflect a variety of Italian cuisines. No other country in the world has a cooking style that incorporates such a wide variety of pastas, cheeses, sauces, and spices. The vast cuisine differences originate from peasant heritage and geographical differences. Italy is home to fertile valleys, mountains covered with forests, cool foothills, naked rocks, Mediterranean coastlines, and arid plains. Different foods originate from these different geographical areas. For example, risotto came from Milan and tortellini from Bologna.

As a peninsula, Italy has been positioned throughout its history to have access to imports of various foods, wheat, wine, and spices from all over the world. You will enjoy a little taste of Italy in each spoonful of the soups that follow.

Minestrone Soup

Ingredients	6-8 Servings	3-4 Servings	1-2 Servings
Celery	4 teaspoons	2 teaspoons	1 teaspoon
Onion	8 teaspoons	4 teaspoons	2 teaspoons
Carrots	4 teaspoons	2 teaspoons	1 teaspoon
Peas	4 teaspoons	2 teaspoons	1 teaspoon
Mixed peppers	2 teaspoons	1 teaspoon	1/2 teaspoon
Spinach	8 teaspoons	4 teaspoons	2 teaspoons
Tomato dices	1/2 cup	1/4 cup	2 TBS
Tomato powder	1/2 cup	1/4 cup	2 TBS
Sugar	2 teaspoons	1 teaspoon	1/2 teaspoon
Diltani pasta	3/4 cup	6 TBS	3 TBS
Parsley	4 teaspoons	2 teaspoons	1 teaspoon
Oregano	1 teaspoon	1/2 teaspoon	1/4 teaspoon
Basil	1 teaspoon	1/2 teaspoon	1/4 teaspoon
Chicken bouillon	2 teaspoons	1 teaspoon	1/2 teaspoon
Navy beans	1 cup	1/2 cup	1/4 cup
Pepper	1/2 teaspoon	1/4 teaspoon	1/8 teaspoon
Salt	1/2 teaspoon	1/4 teaspoon	1/8 teaspoon
Water	8 cups	4 cups	2 cups

Heat the water to boiling, remove from heat, and stir in mix. Cover with a lid, and let the mixture sit for 30 minutes to allow vegetables to hydrate. Bring mixture back to a boil, then turn down the heat, and cook for 30 minutes or until vegetables are tender. Add water if the soup is thicker than desired.

Place water and mix in slow cooker. Turn on high for the first 30 minutes. Add additional water if needed, then turn down to low, and simmer until ready to eat.

Toscana Soup

Ingredients	6-8 Servings	3-4 Servings	1-2 Servings
Onion	1/2 cup	1/4 cup	2 TBS
Potato dices	1 cup	1/2 cup	1/4 cup
Spinach	4 teaspoons	2 teaspoons	1 teaspoon
Cabbage	4 teaspoons	2 teaspoons	1 teaspoon
Leeks	4 teaspoons	2 teaspoons	1 teaspoon
Garlic	4 teaspoons	2 teaspoons	1 teaspoon
TVP ham bits	3/4 cup	6 TBS	3 TBS
Chicken bouillon	2 teaspoons	1 teaspoon	1/2 teaspoon
Water	8 cups	4 cups	2 cups
Pre-cooked spicy sausage links	1 cup	1/2 cup	1/4 cup
Whipped heavy cream (optional)	1 cup	1/2 cup	1/4 cup

Heat the water to boiling, remove from heat, and stir in mix and sausage. Let mixture sit for 30 minutes to allow vegetables to hydrate. Bring mixture back to a boil, and cook for 30 minutes. Top cooked soup with whipped heavy cream, if desired.

Place water and mix and sausage in slow cooker. Turn on high for the first 30 minutes. Turn down to low, and simmer until ready to eat. Top cooked soup with whipped heavy cream, if desired.

Pasta Fagioli Soup

Ingredients	6-8 Servings	3-4 Servings	1-2 Servings
TVP beef bits	1/4 cup	2 TBS	1 TBS
Tomato dices	1/4 cup	2 TBS	1 TBS
Onion	1/4 cup	2 TBS	1 TBS
Celery	4 teaspoons	2 teaspoons	1 teaspoon
Carrots	4 teaspoons	2 teaspoons	1 teaspoon
Cabbage	1/4 cup	2 TBS	1 TBS
Chicken bouillon	2 teaspoons	1 teaspoon	1/2 teaspoon
Beef bouillon	2 teaspoons	1 teaspoon	1/2 teaspoon
Oregano	1 teaspoon	1/2 teaspoon	1/4 teaspoon
Basil	4 teaspoons	2 teaspoons	1 teaspoon
Paprika	1/2 teaspoon	1/4 teaspoon	1/8 teaspoon
Garlic powder	1/2 teaspoon	1/4 teaspoon	1/8 teaspoon
Tomato powder	1/2 cup	1/4 cup	2 TBS
Sugar	2 teaspoons	1 teaspoon	1/2 teaspoon
Kidney beans	1/4 cup	2 TBS	1 TBS
Navy beans	1/4 cup	2 TBS	1 TBS
Pepper	1/2 teaspoon	1/4 teaspoon	1/8 teaspoon
Salt (optional)	1/2 teaspoon	1/4 teaspoon	1/8 teaspoon
Water	8 cups	4 cups	2 cups
Cooked pasta	2 cups	1 cup	1/2 cup
Clamato sauce (optional)	1 can	1/2 can	1/4 can

 Heat the water (and clamato sauce, if desired) to boiling, remove from heat, and stir in mix. Let mixture sit for 30 minutes to allow vegetables to hydrate. Bring mixture back to a boil, and cook for 30 minutes.

 Place water and mix (and clamato sauce, if desired) in slow cooker. Turn on high for the first 30 minutes. Turn down to low, and simmer until ready to eat.

Italian Stew

Ingredients	6-8 Servings	3-4 Servings	1-2 Servings
Small pasta (like orzo)	1 cup	1/2 cup	1/4 cup
Mixed peppers	4 teaspoons	2 teaspoons	1 teaspoon
Onion	1/4 cup	2 TBS	1 TBS
TVP chicken bits	1/2 cup	1/4 cup	2 TBS
Tomato powder	1/2 cup	1/4 cup	2 TBS
Sugar	2 teaspoons	1 teaspoon	1/2 teaspoon
Celery	2 teaspoons	1 teaspoon	1/2 teaspoon
Garlic powder	4 teaspoons	2 teaspoons	1 teaspoon
Oregano	2 teaspoons	1 teaspoon	1/2 teaspoon
Cumin	2 teaspoons	1 teaspoon	1/2 teaspoon
Chicken bouillon	4 teaspoons	2 teaspoons	1 teaspoon
Pepper	2 teaspoons	1 teaspoon	1/2 teaspoon
Salt (optional)	2 teaspoons	1 teaspoon	1/2 teaspoon
Water	8 cups	4 cups	2 cups

Heat the water to boiling, remove from heat, and stir in mix. Cover with a lid, and let the mixture sit for 30 minutes to allow vegetables to hydrate. Bring mixture back to a boil, then turn down the heat, and cook for 30 minutes or until vegetables are tender. Add water if the soup is thicker than desired.

Place water and mix in slow cooker. Turn on high for the first 30 minutes. Add additional water if needed, then turn down to low, and simmer until ready to eat.

Soup Au Pistou

Ingredients	6-8 Servings	3-4 Servings	1-2 Servings
Navy beans	1/2 cup	1/4 cup	2 TBS
Onion	4 teaspoons	2 teaspoons	1 teaspoon
Tomato dices	1/2 cup	1/4 cup	2 TBS
Tomato powder	1/2 cup	1/4 cup	2 TBS
Sugar	2 teaspoons	1 teaspoon	1/2 teaspoon
Basil	4 teaspoons	2 teaspoons	1 teaspoon
Garlic	4 teaspoons	2 teaspoons	1 teaspoon
Leeks	2 teaspoons	1 teaspoon	1/2 teaspoon
Carrots	2 teaspoons	1 teaspoon	1/2 teaspoon
Potato dices	1/2 cup	1/4 cup	2 TBS
Chicken bouillon	4 teaspoons	2 teaspoons	1 teaspoon
TVP chicken bits	1/4 cup	2 TBS	1 TBS
Green beans	4 teaspoons	2 teaspoons	1 teaspoon
Cabbage	4 teaspoons	2 teaspoons	1 teaspoon
Spinach	4 teaspoons	2 teaspoons	1 teaspoon
Mixed peppers	2 teaspoons	1 teaspoon	1/2 teaspoon
Pasta (like star or small)	3/4 cup	6 TBS	3 TBS
Salt (optional)	2 teaspoons	1 teaspoon	1/2 teaspoon
Water	8 cups	4 cups	2 cups
Olive oil	4 teaspoons	2 teaspoons	1 teaspoon
Parmesan cheese	1/2 cup	1/4 cup	2 TBS

Heat the water to boiling, remove from heat and stir in oil and mix. Cover with a lid, and let the mixture sit for 30 minutes to allow vegetables to hydrate. Bring mixture back to a boil, then turn down the heat, and cook for 30 minutes or until vegetables are tender. Add water if the soup is thicker than desired. Top with parmesan cheese before serving.

Place water, oil, and mix in slow cooker. Turn on high for the first 30 minutes. Add additional water if needed, then turn down to low, and simmer until ready to eat. Top with parmesan cheese before serving.

San Marco Soup

Ingredients	6-8 Servings	3-4 Servings	1-2 Servings
Mixed peppers	2 teaspoons	1 teaspoon	1/2 teaspoon
Broccoli	4 teaspoons	2 teaspoons	1 teaspoon
Zucchini	4 teaspoons	2 teaspoons	1 teaspoon
Carrots	4 teaspoons	2 teaspoons	1 teaspoon
Onion	1/3 cup	8 teaspoons	4 teaspoons
Garlic	2 teaspoons	1 teaspoon	1/2 teaspoon
Tomato dices	1/2 cup	1/4 cup	2 TBS
Tomato powder	1/2 cup	1/4 cup	2 TBS
Sugar	4 teaspoons	2 teaspoons	1 teaspoon
Chicken bouillon	4 teaspoons	2 teaspoons	1 teaspoon
TVP chicken chunks	1 cup	1/2 cup	1/4 cup
Italian seasoning	2 teaspoons	1 teaspoon	1/2 teaspoon
Instant potato flakes	4 teaspoons	2 teaspoons	1 teaspoon
Pepper	1/2 teaspoon	1/4 teaspoon	1/8 teaspoon
Salt (optional)	1/2 teaspoon	1/4 teaspoon	1/8 teaspoon
Water	8 cups	4 cups	2 cups
Cooked fettuccini	4 cups	2 cups	1 cup
Oil or butter	4 teaspoons	2 teaspoons	1 teaspoon

Heat the water to boiling, remove from heat. Add oil, and stir in mix. Cover with a lid, and let the mixture sit for 30 minutes to allow vegetables to hydrate. Bring mixture back to a boil, then turn down the heat, and cook for 30 minutes or until vegetables are tender. Add water if the soup is thicker than desired. Stir the drained fettuccini into the cooked mixture before serving.

Place water, oil, and mix in slow cooker. Turn on high for the first 30 minutes. Add additional water if needed, then turn down to low, and simmer until ready to eat. Stir the drained fettuccini into the cooked mixture before serving.

Pasta Primavera

Ingredients	6-8 Servings	3-4 Servings	1-2 Servings
Butter powder	1/2 cup	1/4 cup	2 TBS
Onion	4 teaspoons	2 teaspoons	1 teaspoon
Carrots	4 teaspoons	2 teaspoons	1 teaspoon
Broccoli	1/4 cup	2 TBS	1 TBS
Mushrooms	1/4 cup	2 TBS	1 TBS
Zucchini	4 teaspoons	2 teaspoons	1 teaspoon
Garlic	4 teaspoons	2 teaspoons	1 teaspoon
Beef bouillon	4 teaspoons	2 teaspoons	1 teaspoon
TVP beef bits	1 cup	1/2 cup	1/4 cup
Tomato dices	1/4 cup	2 TBS	1 TBS
Tomato powder	1 cup	1/2 cup	1/4 cup
Parsley	2 teaspoons	1 teaspoon	1/2 teaspoon
Oregano	2 teaspoons	1 teaspoon	1/2 teaspoon
Rosemary	2 teaspoons	1 teaspoon	1/2 teaspoon
Red pepper flakes	1/2 teaspoon	1/4 teaspoon	1/8 teaspoon
Sugar	4 teaspoons	2 teaspoons	1 teaspoon
Pepper	1/2 teaspoon	1/4 teaspoon	1/8 teaspoon
Water	8 cups	4 cups	2 cups
Cooked angel hair pasta	4 cups	2 cups	1 cup
Olive oil	4 teaspoons	2 teaspoons	1 teaspoon
Parmesan cheese	1/2 cup	1/4 cup	2 TBS

Heat the water to boiling, remove from heat, add oil, and stir in mix. Cover with a lid, and let the mixture sit for 30 minutes to allow vegetables to hydrate. Bring mixture back to a boil, then turn down the heat, and cook for 30 minutes or until vegetables are tender. Add water if the soup is thicker than desired. Pour the cooked mixture over drained angel hair pasta and top with Parmesan cheese before serving.

Place water, oil, and mix in slow cooker. Turn on high for the first 30 minutes. Add additional water if needed, then turn down to low, and simmer until ready to eat. Pour the cooked mixture over drained angel hair pasta and top with Parmesan cheese before serving.

Tomato Tortellini Soup

Ingredients	6-8 Servings	3-4 Servings	1-2 Servings
Onion	1/4 cup	2 TBS	1 TBS
Tomato dices	1 cup	1/2 cup	1/4 cup
Chicken bouillon	4 teaspoons	2 teaspoons	1 teaspoon
Tomato powder	1 cup	1/2 cup	1/4 cup
Sugar	4 teaspoons	2 teaspoons	1 teaspoon
Sage	2 teaspoons	1 teaspoon	1/2 teaspoon
Pepper	1/2 teaspoon	1/4 teaspoon	1/8 teaspoon
Salt (optional)	1/2 teaspoon	1/4 teaspoon	1/8 teaspoon
Water	8 cups	4 cups	2 cups
Cooking or olive oil	4 teaspoons	2 teaspoons	1 teaspoon
Cooked tortellini	4 cups	2 cups	1 cup
Parmesan cheese	1/4 cup	2 TBS	1 TBS

Heat the water to boiling, remove from heat, add oil, and stir in mix. Cover with a lid, and let the mixture sit for 30 minutes to allow vegetables to hydrate. Bring mixture back to a boil, then turn down the heat, and cook for 30 minutes or until vegetables are tender. Add water if the soup is thicker than desired.

Place water, oil, and mix in slow cooker. Turn on high for the first 30 minutes. Add additional water if needed, then turn down to low, and simmer until ready to eat.

Blend the cooked mixture in a traditional blender or with a stick blender. Pour mixture over the cooked and drained pasta. Top with the parmesan cheese.

TVP Chicken Tortellini Soup

Ingredients	6-8 Servings	3-4 Servings	1-2 Servings
TVP chicken bits	1 cup	1/2 cup	1/4 cup
Chicken bouillon	4 teaspoons	2 teaspoons	1 teaspoon
White wine powder	1/4 cup	2 TBS	1 TBS
Sour cream powder	1/2 cup	1/4 cup	2 TBS
Mushrooms	1 cup	1/2 cup	1/4 cup
Carrots	4 teaspoons	2 teaspoons	1 teaspoon
Spinach	4 teaspoons	2 teaspoons	1 teaspoon
Broccoli	4 teaspoons	2 teaspoons	1 teaspoon
Cabbage	4 teaspoons	2 teaspoons	1 teaspoon
Tarragon	1 teaspoon	1/2 teaspoon	1/4 teaspoon
Pepper	1/2 teaspoon	1/4 teaspoon	1/8 teaspoon
Salt (optional)	1/2 teaspoon	1/4 teaspoon	1/8 teaspoon
Water	8 cups	4 cups	2 cups
Canola or Olive oil	4 teaspoons	2 teaspoons	1 teaspoon
Cooked cheese-filled tortellini	4 cups	2 cups	1 cup
Parmesan cheese	1/2 cup	1/4 cup	2 TBS

Heat the water to boiling, remove from heat, add oil, and stir in mix. Cover with a lid, and let the mixture sit for 30 minutes to allow vegetables to hydrate. Bring mixture back to a boil, then turn down the heat, and cook for 30 minutes or until vegetables are tender. Add water if the soup is thicker than desired. Stir in the cooked tortellini before serving.

Place water, oil, and mix in slow cooker. Turn on high for the first 30 minutes. Add additional water if needed, then turn down to low, and simmer until ready to eat. Stir in the cooked tortellini before serving.

Italian Vegetable Soup

Ingredients	6-8 Servings	3-4 Servings	1-2 Servings
Onion	1/4 cup	2 TBS	1 TBS
Carrots	4 teaspoons	2 teaspoons	1 teaspoon
Zucchini	4 teaspoons	2 teaspoons	1 teaspoon
Tomato dices	1/4 cup	2 TBS	1 TBS
Tomato powder	1/2 cup	1/4 cup	2 TBS
Sugar	4 teaspoons	2 teaspoons	1 teaspoon
Basil	4 teaspoons	2 teaspoons	1 teaspoon
Garlic	4 teaspoons	2 teaspoons	1 teaspoon
Oregano	4 teaspoons	2 teaspoons	1 teaspoon
TVP chicken bits	1 cup	1/2 cup	1/4 cup
Chicken bouillon	4 teaspoons	2 teaspoons	1 teaspoon
Pepper	1/2 teaspoon	1/4 teaspoon	1/8 teaspoon
Salt (optional)	1/2 teaspoon	1/4 teaspoon	1/8 teaspoon
Water	8 cups	4 cups	2 cups
Olive oil	1/4 cup	2 TBS	1 TBS
Parmesan cheese	1/2 cup	1/4 cup	2 TBS

Heat the water to boiling, remove from heat, add oil, and stir in mix. Cover with a lid, and let the mixture sit for 30 minutes to allow vegetables to hydrate. Bring mixture back to a boil, then turn down the heat, and cook for 30 minutes or until vegetables are tender. Add water if the soup is thicker than desired. Top with parmesan cheese and serve.

Place water, oil, and mix in slow cooker. Turn on high for the first 30 minutes. Add additional water if needed, then turn down to low, and simmer until ready to eat. Top with parmesan cheese and serve.

TVP Beef Italian Vegetable Soup

Ingredients	6-8 Servings	3-4 Servings	1-2 Servings
Leeks	4 teaspoons	2 teaspoons	1 teaspoon
Garlic	4 teaspoons	2 teaspoons	1 teaspoon
Onion	1/4 cup	2 TBS	1 TBS
Zucchini	1/4 cup	2 TBS	1 TBS
Oregano	4 teaspoons	2 teaspoons	1 teaspoon
Basil	4 teaspoons	2 teaspoons	1 teaspoon
Thyme	1 teaspoon	1/2 teaspoon	1/4 teaspoon
TVP beef bits	1/2 cup	1/4 cup	2 TBS
Beef bouillon	4 teaspoons	2 teaspoons	1 teaspoon
Pepper	1/2 teaspoon	1/4 teaspoon	1/8 teaspoon
Salt (optional)	1/2 teaspoon	1/4 teaspoon	1/8 teaspoon
Water	8 cups	4 cups	2 cups
Olive oil	4 teaspoons	2 teaspoons	1 teaspoon
Artichoke hearts packed in water	2 cans	1 can	1/2 can
Cooked egg noodles	4 cups	2 cups	1 cup
Parmesan cheese	1/4 cup	2 TBS	1 TBS

Heat the water to boiling, remove from heat, add oil, and stir in mix. Cover with a lid, and let the mixture sit for 30 minutes to allow vegetables to hydrate. Bring mixture back to a boil, then turn down the heat, and cook for 30 minutes or until vegetables are tender. Add water if the soup is thicker than desired. Add cooked and drained egg noodles, parmesan cheese, and artichoke hearts, and cook for 30 additional minutes.

Place water, oil, and mix in slow cooker. Turn on high for the first 30 minutes. Add artichoke hearts and simmer until ready to eat. Just before serving, stir in the cooked and drained egg noodles and parmesan cheese.

Rigatoni with Vegetable Soup

Ingredients	6-8 Servings	3-4 Servings	1-2 Servings
Mushrooms	1 cup	1/2 cup	1/4 cup
Carrots	4 teaspoons	2 teaspoons	1 teaspoon
Onion	1/4 cup	2 TBS	1 TBS
Mixed peppers	2 teaspoons	1 teaspoon	1/2 teaspoon
Tomato powder	1/2 cup	1/4 cup	2 TBS
Sugar	4 teaspoons	2 teaspoons	1 teaspoon
Red wine powder	1/2 cup	1/4 cup	2 TBS
Thyme	2 teaspoons	1 teaspoon	1/2 teaspoon
Garlic	4 teaspoons	2 teaspoons	1 teaspoon
Oregano	4 teaspoons	2 teaspoons	1 teaspoon
Ground Cloves	1/2 teaspoon	1/4 teaspoon	1/8 teaspoon
Chicken bouillon	4 teaspoons	2 teaspoons	1 teaspoon
White cheese powder	1/4 cup	2 TBS	1 TBS
Sour cream powder	1/4 cup	2 TBS	1 TBS
Dry milk	1/4 cup	2 TBS	1 TBS
Pepper	1/2 teaspoon	1/4 teaspoon	1/8 teaspoon
Salt (optional)	1/2 teaspoon	1/4 teaspoon	1/8 teaspoon
Water	8 cups	4 cups	2 cups
Olive oil	4 teaspoons	2 teaspoons	1 teaspoon
Cooked rigatoni pasta	4 cups	2 cups	1 cup
Parmesan cheese	1/2 cup	1/4 cup	2 TBS

 Heat the water to boiling, remove from heat, add oil, and stir in mix. Cover with a lid, and let the mixture sit for 30 minutes to allow vegetables to hydrate. Bring mixture back to a boil, then turn down the heat, and cook for 30 minutes or until vegetables are tender. Add water if the soup is thicker than desired.

 Place water, oil, and mix in slow cooker. Turn on high for the first 30 minutes. Add additional water if needed, then turn down to low, and simmer until ready to eat.

For a creamy consistency, use a traditional or stick blender and blend to a smooth consistency and pour the mixture over cooked and drained pasta.

Creamy Italian Soup

Ingredients	6-8 Servings	3-4 Servings	1-2 Servings
Onion	1/4 cup	2 TBS	1 TBS
Celery	4 teaspoons	2 teaspoons	1 teaspoon
Garlic	4 teaspoons	2 teaspoons	1 teaspoon
Navy beans	2 cups	1 cup	1/2 cup
Chicken bouillon	4 teaspoons	2 teaspoons	1 teaspoon
Spinach	4 teaspoons	2 teaspoons	1 teaspoon
Thyme	2 teaspoons	1 teaspoon	1/2 teaspoon
Italian seasoning	2 teaspoons	1 teaspoon	1/2 teaspoon
Lemon juice powder	4 teaspoons	2 teaspoons	1 teaspoon
Pepper	1/2 teaspoon	1/4 teaspoon	1/8 teaspoon
Salt (optional)	1/2 teaspoon	1/4 teaspoon	1/8 teaspoon
Water	8 cups	4 cups	2 cups
Canola oil	4 teaspoons	2 teaspoons	1 teaspoon
Parmesan cheese	1/4 cup	2 TBS	1 TBS

Heat the water to boiling, remove from heat, add oil, and stir in mix. Cover with a lid, and let the mixture sit for 30 minutes to allow vegetables to hydrate. Bring mixture back to a boil, then turn down the heat, and cook for 30 minutes or until vegetables are tender. Add water if the soup is thicker than desired.

Place water, oil, and mix in slow cooker. Turn on high for the first 30 minutes. Add additional water if needed, then turn down to low, and simmer until ready to eat.

You may serve the soup as is, or if you desire a creamed soup, use a conventional or stick blender to blend the mixture to a creamy texture. Top with parmesan cheese before serving.

Potato Florentine Soup

Ingredients	6-8 Servings	3-4 Servings	1-2 Servings
TVP chicken bits	1/4 cup	2 TBS	1 TBS
Chicken bouillon	4 teaspoons	2 teaspoons	1 teaspoon
Onion	4 teaspoons	2 teaspoons	1 teaspoon
Garlic	4 teaspoons	2 teaspoons	1 teaspoon
Tomato dices	4 teaspoons	2 teaspoons	1 teaspoon
Tomato powder	4 teaspoons	2 teaspoons	1 teaspoon
Potato dices	1/2 cup	1/4 cup	2 TBS
Spinach	1/2 cup	1/4 cup	2 TBS
Sugar	2 teaspoons	1 teaspoon	1/2 teaspoon
Cream cheese powder	1/4 cup	2 TBS	1 TBS
Vinegar powder	2 teaspoons	1 teaspoon	1/2 teaspoon
Basil	4 teaspoons	2 teaspoons	1 teaspoon
Paprika	1/2 teaspoon	1/4 teaspoon	1/8 teaspoon
Italian seasoning	1 teaspoon	1/2 teaspoon	1/4 teaspoon
Dry milk	8 teaspoons	4 teaspoons	2 teaspoons
Pepper	1/2 teaspoon	1/4 teaspoon	1/8 teaspoon
Salt (optional)	1/2 teaspoon	1/4 teaspoon	1/8 teaspoon
Water	8 cups	4 cups	2 cups

Heat the water to boiling, remove from heat, and stir in mix. Cover with a lid, and let the mixture sit for 30 minutes to allow vegetables to hydrate. Bring mixture back to a boil, then turn down the heat, and cook for 30 minutes or until vegetables are tender. Add water if the soup is thicker than desired.

Place water and mix in slow cooker. Turn on high for the first 30 minutes. Add additional water if needed, then turn down to low, and simmer until ready to eat.

Italian Pasta Vegetable Soup

Ingredients	6-8 Servings	3-4 Servings	1-2 Servings
Onion	8 teaspoons	4 teaspoons	2 teaspoons
Celery	2 teaspoons	1 teaspoon	1/2 teaspoon
Carrots	2 teaspoons	1 teaspoon	1/2 teaspoon
Garlic	4 teaspoons	2 teaspoons	1 teaspoon
Kidney Beans	1/2 cup	1/4 cup	2 TBS
Beef bouillon	4 teaspoons	2 teaspoons	1 teaspoon
TVP beef bits	1/4 cup	2 TBS	1 TBS
Parsley	4 teaspoons	2 teaspoons	1 teaspoon
Oregano	2 teaspoons	1 teaspoon	1/2 teaspoon
Basil	2 teaspoons	1 teaspoon	1/2 teaspoon
Cabbage	4 teaspoons	2 teaspoons	1 teaspoon
Corn	4 teaspoons	2 teaspoons	1 teaspoon
Green beans	4 teaspoons	2 teaspoons	1 teaspoon
Pepper	1/2 teaspoon	1/4 teaspoon	1/8 teaspoon
Salt (optional)	1/2 teaspoon	1/4 teaspoon	1/8 teaspoon
Water	8 cups	4 cups	2 cups
Cooked macaroni	4 cups	2 cups	1 cup
Canola oil	4 teaspoons	2 teaspoons	1 teaspoon
Parmesan cheese	4 TBS	2 TBS	1 TBS

Heat the water to boiling, remove from heat, add oil, and stir in mix. Cover with a lid, and let the mixture sit for 30 minutes to allow vegetables to hydrate. Bring mixture back to a boil, then turn down the heat, and cook for 30 minutes or until vegetables are tender. Add water if the soup is thicker than desired. Mix with cooked macaroni, and top with parmesan cheese before serving.

Place water, oil, and mix in slow cooker. Turn on high for the first 30 minutes. Add additional water if needed, then turn down to low, and simmer until ready to eat. Mix with cooked macaroni, and top with parmesan cheese before serving.

Italian Peasant Soup

Ingredients	6-8 Servings	3-4 Servings	1-2 Servings
Onion	8 teaspoons	4 teaspoons	2 teaspoons
Garlic	4 teaspoons	2 teaspoons	1 teaspoon
Chicken bouillon	4 teaspoons	2 teaspoons	1 teaspoon
TVP beef bits	1/2 cup	1/4 cup	2 TBS
TVP chicken chunks	1/2 cup	1/4 cup	2 TBS
Oregano	2 teaspoons	1 teaspoon	1/2 teaspoon
Basil	4 teaspoons	2 teaspoons	1 teaspoon
Vinegar powder	2 teaspoons	1 teaspoon	1/2 teaspoon
Spinach	8 teaspoons	4 teaspoons	2 teaspoons
Tomato dices	4 teaspoons	2 teaspoons	1 teaspoon
Tomato powder	1/2 cup	1/4 cup	2 TBS
Sugar	4 teaspoons	2 teaspoons	1 teaspoon
Navy beans	1 cup	1/2 cup	1/4 cup
Pepper	1/2 teaspoon	1/4 teaspoon	1/8 teaspoon
Salt (optional)	1/2 teaspoon	1/4 teaspoon	1/8 teaspoon
Water	8 cups	4 cups	2 cups
Canola oil	4 teaspoons	2 teaspoons	1 teaspoon
Parmesan cheese	1/4 cup	2 TBS	1 TBS

Heat the water to boiling, remove from heat, add oil, and stir in mix. Cover with a lid, and let the mixture sit for 30 minutes to allow vegetables to hydrate. Bring mixture back to a boil, then turn down the heat, and cook for 30 minutes or until vegetables are tender. Add water if the soup is thicker than desired. Top with parmesan cheese before serving.

Place water, oil, and mix in slow cooker. Turn on high for the first 30 minutes. Add additional water if needed, then turn down to low, and simmer until ready to eat. Top with parmesan cheese before serving.

Stew & Chowder Mixes

Stews and Chowders

The mixes in this section are for stews and chowders. Chowder is a thick soup that, in addition to a variety of meats and seafood, contains vegetables, such as potatoes and onions, in a milk or tomato base.

A stew, on the other hand, is a dish cooked by stewing (slow cooking or simmering). It is typically a mixture of meat or fish and vegetables with stock.

The recipes in this section utilize TVP (Textured Vegetable Protein) to replicate the heartiness and flavor of meat. Stews and chowders are thick and hearty enough to be a meal by themselves. Mmmmm . . . nothing makes a house smell quite as inviting as when a pot of soup, stew, or chowder is on the stove!

Veggie Chowder

Ingredients	6-8 Servings	3-4 Servings	1-2 Servings
Onion	1/4 cup	2 TBS	1 TBS
Mixed peppers	2 teaspoons	1 teaspoon	1/2 teaspoon
Corn	4 teaspoons	2 teaspoons	1 teaspoon
Green beans	4 teaspoons	2 teaspoons	1 teaspoon
Cabbage	4 teaspoons	2 teaspoons	1 teaspoon
Spinach	4 teaspoons	2 teaspoons	1 teaspoon
Mushrooms	4 teaspoons	2 teaspoons	1 teaspoon
Potato dices	2/3 cup	1/3 cup	3 TBS
Mustard powder	1 teaspoon	1/2 teaspoon	1/4 teaspoon
Dry milk	3/4 cup	6 TBS	3 TBS
Garlic	2 teaspoons	1 teaspoon	1/2 teaspoon
Chicken bouillon	4 teaspoons	2 teaspoons	1 teaspoon
TVP ham bits	1/4 cup	2 TBS	1 TBS
Pepper	1/2 teaspoon	1/4 teaspoon	1/8 teaspoon
Salt	1/2 teaspoon	1/4 teaspoon	1/8 teaspoon
Water	8 cups	4 cups	2 cups water
Canola Oil	4 teaspoons	2 teaspoons	1 teaspoon

 Heat the water to boiling, remove from heat, add oil, and stir in mix. Cover with a lid, and let the mixture sit for 30 minutes to allow vegetables to hydrate. Bring mixture back to a boil, then turn down the heat, and cook for 30 minutes or until vegetables are tender. Add water if the soup is thicker than desired.

Place water, oil, and mix in slow cooker. Turn on high for the first 30 minutes. Add additional water if needed, then turn down to low, and simmer until ready to eat.

TVP Beefy Stew

Ingredients	6-8 Servings	3-4 Servings	1-2 Servings
TVP beef bits	2/3 cup	1/3 cup	8 teaspoons
Mushrooms	1/4 cup	2 TBS	1 TBS
Celery	4 teaspoons	2 teaspoons	1 teaspoon
Onion	1/2 cup	1/4 cup	2 TBS
Beef bouillon	4 teaspoons	2 teaspoons	1 teaspoon
Carrots	4 teaspoons	2 teaspoons	1 teaspoon
Potato dices	1 cup	1/2 cup	1/4 cup
Basil	4 teaspoons	2 teaspoons	1 teaspoon
Pepper	1/2 teaspoon	1/4 teaspoon	1/8 teaspoon
Salt	1/2 teaspoon	1/4 teaspoon	1/8 teaspoon
Water	8 cups	4 cups	2 cups

Heat the water to boiling, remove from heat, and stir in mix. Cover with a lid, and let the mixture sit for 30 minutes to allow vegetables to hydrate. Bring mixture back to a boil, then turn down the heat, and cook for 30 minutes or until vegetables are tender. Add water if the soup is thicker than desired.

Place water and mix in slow cooker. Turn on high for the first 30 minutes. Add additional water if needed, then turn down to low, and simmer until ready to eat.

Mushroom Chowder

Ingredients	6-8 Servings	3-4 Servings	1-2 Servings
Chicken bouillon	2 teaspoons	1 teaspoon	1/2 teaspoon
Butter powder	1/4 cup	2 TBS	1 TBS
Mushrooms	2 cups	1 cup	1/2 cup
Onion	1/4 cup	2 TBS	1 TBS
Soy sauce powder	4 teaspoons	2 teaspoons	1 teaspoon
Pearl couscous	1 cup	1/2 cup	1/4 cup
Water	8 cups	4 cups	2 cups
Olive oil	4 teaspoons	2 teaspoons	1 teaspoon

Heat the water to boiling, remove from heat, add oil, and stir in mix. Cover with a lid, and let the mixture sit for 30 minutes to allow vegetables to hydrate. Bring mixture back to a boil, then turn down the heat, and cook for 30 minutes or until vegetables are tender. Add water if the soup is thicker than desired.

Place water, oil, and mix in slow cooker. Turn on high for the first 30 minutes. Add additional water if needed, then turn down to low, and simmer until ready to eat.

Mushroom Orzo Soup

Ingredients	6-8 Servings	3-4 Servings	1-2 Servings
Chicken bouillon	4 teaspoons	2 teaspoons	1 teaspoon
Onion	4 teaspoons	2 teaspoons	1 teaspoon
Cabbage	4 teaspoons	2 teaspoons	1 teaspoon
Spinach	4 teaspoons	2 teaspoons	1 teaspoon
Mushrooms	1 cup	1/2 cup	1/4 cup
Orzo pasta	1 cup	1/2 cup	1/4 cup
Red wine powder	1/4 cup	2 TBS	1 TBS
Vinegar powder	4 teaspoons	2 teaspoons	1 teaspoon
Butter powder	1/4 cup	2 TBS	1 TBS
White cheese powder	1/4 cup	2 TBS	1 TBS
Pepper	1/2 teaspoon	1/4 teaspoon	1/8 teaspoon
Salt (optional)	1/2 teaspoon	1/4 teaspoon	1/8 teaspoon
Water	8 cups	4 cups	2 cups
Olive oil	4 teaspoons	2 teaspoons	1 teaspoon

Heat the water to boiling, remove from heat, add oil, and stir in mix. Cover with a lid, and let the mixture sit for 30 minutes to allow vegetables to hydrate. Bring mixture back to a boil, then turn down the heat, and cook for 30 minutes or until vegetables are tender. Add water if the soup is thicker than desired.

Place water, oil, and mix in slow cooker. Turn on high for the first 30 minutes. Add additional water if needed, then turn down to low, and simmer until ready to eat.

Creamy Green Stew

Ingredients	6-8 Servings	3-4 Servings	1-2 Servings
Onion	1/4 cup	2 TBS	1 TBS
Leeks	1/4 cup	2 TBS	1 TBS
Spinach	1/4 cup	2 TBS	1 TBS
Broccoli	1/4 cup	2 TBS	1 TBS
Potato dices	1 cup	1/2 cup	1/4 cup
Butter powder	1/4 cup	2 TBS	1 TBS
All purpose flour	4 teaspoons	2 teaspoons	1 teaspoon
Nutmeg	1/4 teaspoon	1/8 teaspoon	1 dash
Red pepper flakes	1/4 teaspoon	1/8 teaspoon	1 dash
Lemon peel	1 teaspoon	1/2 teaspoon	1/4 teaspoon
Dry milk	1 cup	1/2 cup	1/4 cup
Pepper	1/2 teaspoon	1/4 teaspoon	1/8 teaspoon
Salt (optional)	1/2 teaspoon	1/4 teaspoon	1/8 teaspoon
Water	8 cups	4 cups	2 cups

 Heat the water to boiling, remove from heat, and stir in mix. Cover with a lid, and let the mixture sit for 30 minutes to allow vegetables to hydrate. Bring mixture back to a boil, then turn down the heat, and cook for 30 minutes or until vegetables are tender. Add water if the soup is thicker than desired.

 Place water and mix in slow cooker. Turn on high for the first 30 minutes. Add additional water if needed, then turn down to low, and simmer until ready to eat.

For a creamy consistency, use a traditional or stick blender and blend to a smooth consistency before serving.

Mulligan Stew

Ingredients	6-8 Servings	3-4 Servings	1-2 Servings
Apple dices	1/3 cup	8 teaspoons	4 teaspoons
Carrots	4 teaspoons	2 teaspoons	1 teaspoon
Tomato dices	1/3 cup	8 teaspoons	4 teaspoons
Celery	4 teaspoons	2 teaspoons	1 teaspoon
Long grain rice	2/3 cup	1/3 cup	8 teaspoons
Onion	4 teaspoons	2 teaspoons	1 teaspoon
Raisins	1/4 cup	2 TBS	1 TBS
Parsley	4 teaspoons	2 teaspoons	1 teaspoon
Curry powder	1 teaspoon	1/2 teaspoon	1/4 teaspoon
Lemon peel	1 teaspoon	1/2 teaspoon	1/4 teaspoon
Nutmeg	1/4 teaspoon	1/8 teaspoon	1 dash
Chicken bouillon	4 teaspoons	2 teaspoons	1 teaspoon
TVP chicken chunks	1/2 cup	1/4 cup	2 TBS
Pepper	1/2 teaspoon	1/4 teaspoon	1/8 teaspoon
Salt (optional)	1/2 teaspoon	1/4 teaspoon	1/8 teaspoon
Water	8 cups	4 cups	2 cups

Heat the water to boiling, remove from heat, and stir in mix. Cover with a lid, and let the mixture sit for 30 minutes to allow vegetables to hydrate. Bring mixture back to a boil, then turn down the heat, and cook for 30 minutes or until vegetables are tender. Add water if the soup is thicker than desired.

Place water and mix in slow cooker. Turn on high for the first 30 minutes. Add additional water if needed, then turn down to low, and simmer until ready to eat.

50

Mexican Corn Chowder

Ingredients	6-8 Servings	3-4 Servings	1-2 Servings
Corn	1 cup	1/2 cup	1/4 cup
Potato dices	1 cup	1/2 cup	1/4 cup
Onion	1/4 cup	2 TBS	1 TBS
Mixed peppers	2 teaspoons	1 teaspoon	1/2 teaspoon
Dry milk	1/2 cup	1/4 cup	2 TBS
All purpose flour	1/4 cup	2 TBS	1 TBS
Cumin	1 TBS	1 1/2 teaspoon	3/4 teaspoon
Garlic	1 teaspoon	1/2 teaspoon	1/4 teaspoon
Parsley	1 TBS	1 1/2 teaspoon	3/4 teaspoon
Jalapeño	1/2 teaspoon	1/4 teaspoon	1/8 teaspoon
Chicken bouillon	2 teaspoons	1 teaspoon	1/2 teaspoon
Pepper	1/2 teaspoon	1/4 teaspoon	1/8 teaspoon
Salt (optional)	1 teaspoon	1/2 teaspoon	1/4 teaspoon
Water	8 cups	4 cups	2 cups

Heat the water to boiling, remove from heat, and stir in mix. Cover with a lid, and let the mixture sit for 30 minutes to allow vegetables to hydrate. Bring mixture back to a boil, then turn down the heat, and cook for 30 minutes or until vegetables are tender. Add water if the soup is thicker than desired.

Place water and mix in slow cooker. Turn on high for the first 30 minutes. Add additional water if needed, then turn down to low, and simmer until ready to eat.

Chicken-Flavored Soup Mixes

Chicken-Flavored Soups

The soup mixes in this section are all chicken-flavored soups. While most of the soups here are hearty enough to be a meal, they are still light enough to be eaten any time of year.

Most of us associate chicken-flavored soups with "comfort food." At one time or another in our lives, we have been nursed back to health by chicken soup.

The "chicken" in these mixes are TVP chicken bits (with the texture of ground chicken) or TVP chicken chunks (the texture of small bites of chicken). Here's to your enjoying one of these soups when you are feeling well and not just when you are sick.

TVP Chicken Noodle Soup

Ingredients	6-8 Servings	3-4 Servings	1-2 Servings
Fine egg noodles	1 cup	1/2 cup	1/4 cup
Chicken bouillon	2 teaspoons	1 teaspoon	1/2 teaspoon
Thyme	1/2 teaspoon	1/4 teaspoon	1/8 teaspoon
Basil	2 teaspoons	1 teaspoon	1/2 teaspoon
Parsley	4 teaspoons	2 teaspoons	1 teaspoon
Celery	2 teaspoons	1 teaspoon	1/2 teaspoon
Carrots	2 teaspoons	1 teaspoon	1/2 teaspoon
Onion	8 teaspoons	4 teaspoons	2 teaspoons
Garlic	2 teaspoons	1 teaspoon	1/2 teaspoon
Chives	2 teaspoons	1 teaspoon	1/2 teaspoon
TVP chicken chunks	1 cup	1/2 cup	1/4 cup
Pepper	1/2 teaspoon	1/4 teaspoon	1/8 teaspoon
Salt	1/2 teaspoon	1/4 teaspoon	1/8 teaspoon
Water	8 cups	4 cups	2 cups

Heat the water to boiling, remove from heat, and stir in mix. Cover with a lid, and let the mixture sit for 30 minutes to allow vegetables to hydrate. Bring mixture back to a boil, then turn down the heat, and cook for 30 minutes or until vegetables are tender. Add water if the soup is thicker than desired.

Place water and mix in slow cooker. Turn on high for the first 30 minutes. Add additional water if needed, then turn down to low, and simmer until ready to eat.

TVP Chicken Soup

Ingredients	6-8 Servings	3-4 Servings	1-2 Servings
Chicken bouillon	2 teaspoons	1 teaspoon	1/2 teaspoon
Onion	1/4 cup	2 TBS	1 TBS
Carrots	8 teaspoons	4 teaspoons	2 teaspoons
Garlic	4 teaspoons	2 teaspoons	1 teaspoon
Sage	1 teaspoon	1/2 teaspoon	1/4 teaspoon
TVP chicken bits	1/4 cup	2 TBS	1 TBS
Small pasta	2 cups	1 cup	1/2 cup
Pepper	1/2 teaspoon	1/4 teaspoon	1/8 teaspoon
Salt	1/2 teaspoon	1/4 teaspoon	1/8 teaspoon
Water	8 cups	4 cups	2 cups
Olive oil	4 teaspoons	2 teaspoons	1 teaspoon

Heat the water to boiling, remove from heat, add oil, and stir in mix. Cover with a lid, and let the mixture sit for 30 minutes to allow vegetables to hydrate. Bring mixture back to a boil, then turn down the heat, and cook for 30 minutes or until vegetables are tender. Add water if the soup is thicker than desired.

Place water, oil, and mix in slow cooker. Turn on high for the first 30 minutes. Add additional water if needed, then turn down to low, and simmer until ready to eat.

TVP Chicken Soup II

Ingredients	6-8 Servings	3-4 Servings	1-2 Servings
Chicken bouillon	4 teaspoons	2 teaspoons	1 teaspoon
Thyme	1 teaspoon	1/2 teaspoon	1/4 teaspoon
Celery	4 teaspoons	2 teaspoons	1 teaspoon
Garlic powder	2 teaspoons	1 teaspoon	1/2 teaspoon
Carrots	4 teaspoons	2 teaspoons	1 teaspoon
Onion	1/4 cup	2 TBS	1 TBS
TVP chicken chunks	1/2 cup	1/4 cup	2 TBS
Fine egg noodles	2 cups	1 cup	1/2 cup
Pepper	1/2 teaspoon	1/4 teaspoon	1/8 teaspoon
Salt	1/2 teaspoon	1/4 teaspoon	1/8 teaspoon
Water	8 cups	4 cups	2 cups

Heat the water to boiling, remove from heat, and stir in mix. Cover with a lid, and let the mixture sit for 30 minutes to allow vegetables to hydrate. Bring mixture back to a boil, then turn down the heat, and cook for 30 minutes or until vegetables are tender. Add water if the soup is thicker than desired.

Place water and mix in slow cooker. Turn on high for the first 30 minutes. Add additional water if needed, then turn down to low, and simmer until ready to eat.

Spicy TVP Chicken Noodle Soup

Ingredients	6-8 Servings	3-4 Servings	1-2 Servings
Onion	1/2 cup	1/4 cup	2 TBS
Soy sauce powder	4 teaspoons	2 teaspoons	1 teaspoon
Garlic powder	4 teaspoons	2 teaspoons	1 teaspoon
Ginger	2 teaspoons	1 teaspoon	1/2 teaspoon
Cinnamon	1/2 teaspoon	1/4 teaspoon	1/8 teaspoon
Cloves	1/2 teaspoon	1/4 teaspoon	1/8 teaspoon
Mixed peppers	1 teaspoon	1/2 teaspoon	1/4 teaspoon
Cabbage	4 teaspoons	2 teaspoons	1 teaspoon
Spinach	4 teaspoons	2 teaspoons	1 teaspoon
Broccoli	4 teaspoons	2 teaspoons	1 teaspoon
Carrots	4 teaspoons	2 teaspoons	1 teaspoon
Chicken bouillon	4 teaspoons	2 teaspoons	1 teaspoon
Cumin	2 teaspoons	1 teaspoon	1/2 teaspoon
Small egg noodles	1 cup	1/2 cup	1/4 cup
TVP chicken chunks	1 cup	1/2 cup	1/4 cup
Pepper	1/2 teaspoon	1/4 teaspoon	1/8 teaspoon
Water	8 cups	4 cups	2 cups

Heat the water to boiling, remove from heat, and stir in mix. Cover with a lid, and let the mixture sit for 30 minutes to allow vegetables to hydrate. Bring mixture back to a boil, then turn down the heat, and cook for 30 minutes or until vegetables are tender. Add water if the soup is thicker than desired.

Place water and mix in slow cooker. Turn on high for the first 30 minutes. Add additional water if needed, then turn down to low, and simmer until ready to eat.

Dilly TVP Chicken Noodle Soup

Ingredients	6-8 Servings	3-4 Servings	1-2 Servings
Carrots	4 teaspoons	2 teaspoons	1 teaspoon
Celery	4 teaspoons	2 teaspoons	1 teaspoon
Ginger	1 teaspoon	1/2 teaspoon	1/4 teaspoon
Cloves	1 teaspoon	1/2 teaspoon	1/4 teaspoon
Garlic powder	4 teaspoons	2 teaspoons	1 teaspoon
Sugar	4 teaspoons	2 teaspoons	1 teaspoon
Dill	2 teaspoons	1 teaspoon	1/2 teaspoon
Chicken bouillon	2 teaspoons	1 teaspoon	1/2 teaspoon
Lemon peel	1/2 teaspoon	1/4 teaspoon	1/8 teaspoon
Small egg noodles	1 cup	1/2 cup	1/4 cup
TVP chicken chunks	1 cup	1/2 cup	1/4 cup
Pepper	1/2 teaspoon	1/4 teaspoon	1/8 teaspoon
Salt (optional)	1 teaspoon	1/2 teaspoon	1/4 teaspoon
Water	8 cups	4 cups	2 cups

Heat the water to boiling, remove from heat, and stir in mix. Cover with a lid, and let the mixture sit for 30 minutes to allow vegetables to hydrate. Bring mixture back to a boil, then turn down the heat, and cook for 30 minutes or until vegetables are tender. Add water if the soup is thicker than desired.

Place water and mix in slow cooker. Turn on high for the first 30 minutes. Add additional water if needed, then turn down to low, and simmer until ready to eat.

Old-Fashioned Chicken Noodle Soup

Ingredients	6-8 Servings	3-4 Servings	1-2 Servings
Carrots	4 teaspoons	2 teaspoons	1 teaspoon
Celery	4 teaspoons	2 teaspoons	1 teaspoon
Onion	4 teaspoons	2 teaspoons	1 teaspoon
Butter powder	1/4 cup	2 TBS	1 TBS
Chicken bouillon	2 teaspoons	1 teaspoon	1/2 teaspoon
Wide egg noodles	1 cup	1/2 cup	1/4 cup
TVP chicken chunks	1 cup	1/2 cup	1/4 cup
Pepper	1/2 teaspoon	1/4 teaspoon	1/8 teaspoon
Salt (optional)	1 teaspoon	1/2 teaspoon	1/4 teaspoon
Water	8 cups	4 cups	2 cups

Heat the water to boiling, remove from heat, and stir in mix. Cover with a lid, and let the mixture sit for 30 minutes to allow vegetables to hydrate. Bring mixture back to a boil, then turn down the heat, and cook for 30 minutes or until vegetables are tender. Add water if the soup is thicker than desired.

Place water and mix in slow cooker. Turn on high for the first 30 minutes. Add additional water if needed, then turn down to low, and simmer until ready to eat.

Barley Soup Mixes

Barley

The soup mixes in this section are all based on barley. Nutritionists recommend at least three servings of whole-grain foods each day. Whole grain barley is a healthy high-fiber, high-protein whole grain boasting numerous health benefits. When cooked, barley has a chewy texture and nutty flavor, similar to brown rice.

Barley's nutrients and high-fiber content have positive effects on:

- lowering cholesterol.
- promoting intestinal health.
- preventing blood sugar levels from rising too high in people with diabetes.
- providing protection against atherosclerosis.
- providing protection against cancers and heart disease.
- supporting cardiovascular health in post-menopausal women.
- substantially lowering the risk of type 2 diabetes.
- providing protection against post-menopausal breast cancer.
- lowering the risk of gallstones.
- reducing the risk of childhood asthma.
- providing copper reducing the symptoms of rheumatoid arthritis.
- supporting development and repair of body tissue.

TVP Beef Barley Soup

Ingredients	6-8 Servings	3-4 Servings	1-2 Servings
Carrots	2 teaspoons	1 teaspoon	1/2 teaspoon
Celery	2 teaspoons	1 teaspoon	1/2 teaspoon
Onion	1/2 cup	1/4 cup	2 TBS
Mushrooms	1/2 cup	1/4 cup	2 TBS
Tomato powder	1/2 cup	1/4 cup	2 TBS
Sugar	2 teaspoons	1 teaspoon	1/2 teaspoon
Garlic	4 teaspoons	2 teaspoons	1 teaspoon
Rosemary	1 teaspoon	1/2 teaspoon	1/4 teaspoon
Beef bouillon	4 teaspoons	2 teaspoons	1 teaspoon
Lemon peel	1/2 teaspoon	1/4 teaspoon	1/8 teaspoon
Pearl barley	1/2 cup	1/4 cup	2 TBS
TVP beef bits	1/2 cup	1/4 cup	2 TBS
Pepper	1/2 teaspoon	1/4 teaspoon	1/8 teaspoon
Salt (optional)	1/2 teaspoon	1/4 teaspoon	1/8 teaspoon
Water	8 cups	4 cups	2 cups

Heat the water to boiling, remove from heat, and stir in mix. Cover with a lid, and let the mixture sit for 30 minutes to allow vegetables to hydrate. Bring mixture back to a boil, then turn down the heat, and cook for 30 - 45 minutes or until vegetables are tender and barley is done to taste. Add water if the soup is thicker than desired.

Place water and mix in slow cooker. Turn on high for the first 30 minutes. Add additional water if needed, then turn down to low, and simmer until ready to eat.

Barley Mushroom Soup

Ingredients	6-8 Servings	3-4 Servings	1-2 Servings
Onion	1/3 cup	8 teaspoons	4 teaspoons
Mushrooms	1 cup	1/2 cup	1/4 cup
Garlic	4 teaspoons	2 teaspoons	1 teaspoon
Chicken bouillon	4 teaspoons	2 teaspoons	1 teaspoon
Pearl barley	1/2 cup	1/4 cup	2 TBS
Spinach	4 teaspoons	2 teaspoons	1 teaspoon
Broccoli	4 teaspoons	2 teaspoons	1 teaspoon
Parsley	1 teaspoon	1/2 teaspoon	1/4 teaspoon
Thyme	1/2 teaspoon	1/4 teaspoon	1/8 teaspoon
Pepper	1/2 teaspoon	1/4 teaspoon	1/8 teaspoon
Salt (optional)	1/2 teaspoon	1/4 teaspoon	1/8 teaspoon
Water	8 cups	4 cups	2 cups
Canola oil	4 teaspoons	2 teaspoons	1 teaspoon

Heat the water to boiling, remove from heat, and stir in mix. Cover with a lid, and let the mixture sit for 30 minutes to allow vegetables to hydrate. Bring mixture back to a boil, then turn down the heat, and cook for 30 - 45 minutes or until vegetables are tender and barley is done to taste. Add water if the soup is thicker than desired.

Place water, oil, and mix in slow cooker. Turn on high for the first 30 minutes. Add additional water if needed, then turn down to low, and simmer until ready to eat.

Barley Vegetable Soup

Ingredients	6-8 Servings	3-4 Servings	1-2 Servings
Onion	1 cup	2 TBS	1 TBS
Mushrooms	1/4 cup	2 TBS	1 TBS
Carrots	4 teaspoons	2 teaspoons	1 teaspoon
Celery	4 teaspoons	2 teaspoons	1 teaspoon
Mixed peppers	1 teaspoon	1/2 teaspoon	1/4 teaspoon
Garlic	4 teaspoons	2 teaspoons	1 teaspoon
Chicken bouillon	4 teaspoons	2 teaspoons	1 teaspoon
Pearl barley	1/2 cup	1/4 cup	2 TBS
Corn	1/2 cup	1/4 cup	2 TBS
Tomato dices	1/2 cup	1/4 cup	2 TBS
Tomato powder	4 teaspoons	2 teaspoons	1 teaspoon
Sugar	2 teaspoons	1 teaspoon	1/2 teaspoon
Italian seasoning	4 teaspoons	2 teaspoons	1 teaspoon
Basil	1 teaspoon	1/2 teaspoon	1/4 teaspoon
Pepper	1/2 teaspoon	1/4 teaspoon	1/8 teaspoon
Salt (optional)	1/2 teaspoon	1/4 teaspoon	1/8 teaspoon
Water	8 cups	4 cups	2 cups
Olive oil	4 teaspoons	2 teaspoons	1 teaspoon

Heat the water to boiling, remove from heat, and stir in mix. Cover with a lid, and let the mixture sit for 30 minutes to allow vegetables to hydrate. Bring mixture back to a boil, then turn down the heat, and cook for 30 - 45 minutes or until vegetables are tender and barley is done to taste. Add water if the soup is thicker than desired.

Place water, oil, and mix in slow cooker. Turn on high for the first 30 minutes. Add additional water if needed, then turn down to low, and simmer until ready to eat.

TVP Beef Potato Barley Soup

Ingredients	6-8 Servings	3-4 Servings	1-2 Servings
Onion	1/3 cup	8 teaspoons	4 teaspoons
Mushrooms	4 teaspoons	2 teaspoons	1 teaspoon
Carrots	4 teaspoons	2 teaspoons	1 teaspoon
Celery	4 teaspoons	2 teaspoons	1 teaspoon
Potato dices	1/3 cup	8 teaspoons	4 teaspoons
Pearl barley	1/2 cup	1/4 cup	2 TBS
Thyme	1 teaspoon	1/2 teaspoon	1/4 teaspoon
TVP beef bits	1/3 cup	8 teaspoons	4 teaspoons
Beef bouillon	4 teaspoons	2 teaspoons	1 teaspoon
Pepper	1/2 teaspoon	1/4 teaspoon	1/8 teaspoon
Salt (optional)	1/2 teaspoon	1/4 teaspoon	1/8 teaspoon
Water	8 cups	4 cups	2 cups
Canola oil	4 teaspoons	2 teaspoons	1 teaspoon

Heat the water to boiling, remove from heat, and stir in mix. Cover with a lid, and let the mixture sit for 30 minutes to allow vegetables to hydrate. Bring mixture back to a boil, then turn down the heat, and cook for 30 - 45 minutes or until vegetables are tender and barley is done to taste. Add water if the soup is thicker than desired.

Place water, oil, and mix in slow cooker. Turn on high for the first 30 minutes. Add additional water if needed, then turn down to low, and simmer until ready to eat.

TVP Beef Tomato Barley Soup

Ingredients	6-8 Servings	3-4 Servings	1-2 Servings
Onion	1/4 cup	2 TBS	1 TBS
Celery	4 teaspoons	2 teaspoons	1 teaspoon
Carrots	4 teaspoons	2 teaspoons	1 teaspoon
Tomato dices	1/3 cup	8 teaspoons	4 teaspoons
Tomato powder	4 teaspoons	2 teaspoons	1 teaspoon
Sugar	2 teaspoons	1 teaspoon	1/2 teaspoon
Pearl barley	1/2 cup	1/4 cup	2 TBS
Beef bouillon	4 teaspoons	2 teaspoons	1 teaspoon
TVP beef bits	1/3 cup	8 teaspoons	4 teaspoons
Parsley	1/4 cup	2 TBS	1 TBS
Pepper	1/2 teaspoon	1/4 teaspoon	1/8 teaspoon
Salt (optional)	1/2 teaspoon	1/4 teaspoon	1/8 teaspoon
Water	8 cups	4 cups	2 cups
Canola oil	4 teaspoons	2 teaspoons	1 teaspoon

Heat the water to boiling, remove from heat, and stir in mix. Cover with a lid, and let the mixture sit for 30 minutes to allow vegetables to hydrate. Bring mixture back to a boil, then turn down the heat, and cook for 30 - 45 minutes or until vegetables are tender and barley is done to taste. Add water if the soup is thicker than desired.

Place water, oil, and mix in slow cooker. Turn on high for the first 30 minutes. Add additional water if needed, then turn down to low, and simmer until ready to eat.

Hearty Mushroom Barley Soup

Ingredients	6-8 Servings	3-4 Servings	1-2 Servings
Onion	4 teaspoons	2 teaspoons	1 teaspoon
Carrots	4 teaspoons	2 teaspoons	1 teaspoon
Mushrooms	1/4 cup	2 TBS	1 TBS
Garlic	4 teaspoons	2 teaspoons	1 teaspoon
Chicken bouillon	4 teaspoons	2 teaspoons	1 teaspoon
Pearl barley	1/2 cup	1/4 cup	2 TBS
Tomato powder	1/2 cup	1/4 cup	2 TBS
Sugar	2 teaspoons	1 teaspoon	1/2 teaspoon
Basil	4 teaspoons	2 teaspoons	1 teaspoon
Italian seasoning	4 teaspoons	2 teaspoons	1 teaspoon
Sour cream powder	1/4 cup	2 TBS	1 TBS
Pepper	1/2 teaspoon	1/4 teaspoon	1/8 teaspoon
Salt (optional)	1/2 teaspoon	1/4 teaspoon	1/8 teaspoon
Water	8 cups	4 cups	2 cups
Canola oil	4 teaspoons	2 teaspoons	1 teaspoon

Heat the water to boiling, remove from heat, and stir in mix. Cover with a lid, and let the mixture sit for 30 minutes to allow vegetables to hydrate. Bring mixture back to a boil, then turn down the heat, and cook for 30 - 45 minutes or until vegetables are tender and barley is done to taste. Add water if the soup is thicker than desired.

Place water, oil, and mix in slow cooker. Turn on high for the first 30 minutes. Add additional water if needed, then turn down to low, and simmer until ready to eat.

Italian Barley Soup

Ingredients	6-8 Servings	3-4 Servings	1-2 Servings
Onion	4 teaspoons	2 teaspoons	1 teaspoon
TVP beef bits	1/2 cup	1/4 cup	2 TBS
Beef bouillon	4 teaspoons	2 teaspoons	1 teaspoon
Pearl barley	1/2 cup	1/4 cup	2 TBS
Tomato powder	1/2 cup	1/4 cup	2 TBS
Sugar	2 teaspoons	1 teaspoon	1/2 teaspoon
Italian seasoning	4 teaspoons	2 teaspoons	1 teaspoon
Pepper	1/2 teaspoon	1/4 teaspoon	1/8 teaspoon
Salt (optional)	1/2 teaspoon	1/4 teaspoon	1/8 teaspoon
Water	8 cups	4 cups	2 cups
Canola oil	4 teaspoons	2 teaspoons	1 teaspoon

Heat the water to boiling, remove from heat, and stir in mix. Cover with a lid, and let the mixture sit for 30 minutes to allow vegetables to hydrate. Bring mixture back to a boil, then turn down the heat, and cook for 30 - 45 minutes or until vegetables are tender and barley is done to taste. Add water if the soup is thicker than desired.

Place water, oil, and mix in slow cooker. Turn on high for the first 30 minutes. Add additional water if needed, then turn down to low, and simmer until ready to eat.

Mexican Bean and Barley Soup

Ingredients	6-8 Servings	3-4 Servings	1-2 Servings
Onion	4 teaspoons	2 teaspoons	1 teaspoon
Garlic	4 teaspoons	2 teaspoons	1 teaspoon
Carrots	4 teaspoons	2 teaspoons	1 teaspoon
Potato dices	1/4 cup	2 TBS	1 TBS
Jalapeño	2 teaspoons	1 teaspoon	1/2 teaspoon
Cumin	2 teaspoons	1 teaspoon	1/2 teaspoon
Coriander	1/2 teaspoon	1/4 teaspoon	1/8 teaspoon
Beef bouillon	4 teaspoons	2 teaspoons	1 teaspoon
Pearl barley	1/2 cup	1/4 cup	2 TBS
Pinto beans	1 cup	1/2 cup	1/4 cup
Lemon juice powder	2 teaspoons	1 teaspoon	1/2 teaspoon
Pepper	1/2 teaspoon	1/4 teaspoon	1/8 teaspoon
Salt (optional)	1/2 teaspoon	1/4 teaspoon	1/8 teaspoon
Water	8 cups	4 cups	2 cups
Canola oil	4 teaspoons	2 teaspoons	1 teaspoon

Heat the water to boiling, remove from heat, and stir in mix. Cover with a lid, and let the mixture sit for 30 minutes to allow vegetables to hydrate. Bring mixture back to a boil, then turn down the heat, and cook for 30 - 45 minutes or until vegetables are tender and barley is done to taste. Add water if the soup is thicker than desired.

Place water, oil, and mix in slow cooker. Turn on high for the first 30 minutes. Add additional water if needed, then turn down to low, and simmer until ready to eat.

Chili Mixes

Chili

The mixes in this section contain a variety of chilis. Chili is one of those dishes that stirs up a lot of passion because of its spice. Traditional versions are made using chili peppers, garlic, onions, and cumin, along with chopped or ground beef. Beans and tomatoes are frequently included.

Variations, both geographic and personal, may involve different types of meat as well as a variety of other ingredients. The chili recipes in this section include vegetarian, chili verde, black bean, red bean, and white bean varieties. Technically, these are all vegetarian chilis because the recipes substitute beef and chicken with TVP. However, in some cases, beef or chicken bouillon have been added to enhance the flavor.

TVP Beef and Bean Chili Verde

Ingredients	6-8 Servings	3-4 Servings	1-2 Servings
TVP beef bits	1 cup	1/2 cup	1/4 cup
Beef bouillon	2 teaspoons	1 teaspoon	1/2 teaspoon
Tomato dices	4 teaspoons	2 teaspoons	1 teaspoon
Tomato powder	1 cup	1/2 cup	1/4 cup
Sugar	4 teaspoons	2 teaspoons	1 teaspoon
Vinegar powder	4 teaspoons	2 teaspoons	1 teaspoon
Mixed peppers	2 teaspoons	1 teaspoon	1/2 teaspoon
Onion	4 teaspoons	2 teaspoons	1 teaspoon
Garlic	4 teaspoons	2 teaspoons	1 teaspoon
Chili powder	4 teaspoons	2 teaspoons	1 teaspoon
Cumin	2 teaspoons	1 teaspoon	1/2 teaspoon
Cayenne pepper	1/4 teaspoon	1/8 teaspoon	1 dash
Pinto beans	1 cup	1/2 cup	1/4 cup
Water	8 cups	4 cups	2 cups

Heat the water to boiling, remove from heat, and stir in mix. Cover with a lid, and let the mixture sit for 30 minutes to allow vegetables to hydrate. Bring mixture back to a boil, then turn down the heat, and cook for 30 minutes or until vegetables are tender. Add water if the soup is thicker than desired.

Place water, oil, and mix in slow cooker. Turn on high for the first 30 minutes. Add additional water if needed, then turn down to low, and simmer until ready to eat.

Veggie Chili

Ingredients	6-8 Servings	3-4 Servings	1-2 Servings
Garlic	4 teaspoons	2 teaspoons	1 teaspoon
Onion	4 teaspoons	2 teaspoons	1 teaspoon
Cumin	4 teaspoons	2 teaspoons	1 teaspoon
Oregano	4 teaspoons	2 teaspoons	1 teaspoon
Celery	4 teaspoons	2 teaspoons	1 teaspoon
Mixed peppers	4 teaspoons	2 teaspoons	1 teaspoon
Jalapeño	2 teaspoons	1 teaspoon	1/2 teaspoon
TVP beef bits	1/2 cup	1/4 cup	2 TBS
Tomato dices	1/2 cup	1/4 cup	2 TBS
Tomato powder	1/4 cup	2 TBS	1 TBS
Sugar	2 TBS	1 TBS	1 teaspoon
Chili powder	8 teaspoons	4 teaspoons	2 teaspoons
Kidney beans	8 teaspoons	4 teaspoons	2 teaspoons
Garbanzo beans	8 teaspoons	4 teaspoons	2 teaspoons
Black beans	8 teaspoons	4 teaspoons	2 teaspoons
Corn	8 teaspoons	4 teaspoons	2 teaspoons
Pepper	1/2 teaspoon	1/4 teaspoon	1/8 teaspoon
Salt (optional)	1/2 teaspoon	1/4 teaspoon	1/8 teaspoon
Water	8 cups	4 cups	2 cups
Olive oil	4 teaspoons	2 teaspoons	1 teaspoon

Heat the water to boiling, remove from heat, add oil, and stir in mix. Cover with a lid, and let the mixture sit for 30 minutes to allow vegetables to hydrate. Bring mixture back to a boil, then turn down the heat, and cook for 30 minutes or until vegetables are tender. Add water if the soup is thicker than desired.

Place water, oil, and mix in slow cooker. Turn on high for the first 30 minutes. Add additional water if needed, then turn down to low, and simmer until ready to eat.

Vegan Pinto Bean Chili

Ingredients	6-8 Servings	3-4 Servings	1-2 Servings
Onion	1/4 cup	2 TBS	1 TBS
Celery	2 teaspoons	1 teaspoon	1/2 teaspoon
Cumin	2 TBS	1 TBS	1 teaspoon
All purpose flour	4 teaspoons	2 teaspoons	1 teaspoon
TVP taco bits	1 cup	1/2 cup	1/4 cup
Tomato dices	1/4 cup	2 TBS	1 TBS
Tomato powder	1/4 cup	2 TBS	1 TBS
Sugar	4 teaspoons	2 teaspoons	1 teaspoon
Chili powder	4 teaspoons	2 teaspoons	1 teaspoon
Vinegar powder	2 teaspoons	1 teaspoon	1/2 teaspoon
Pinto beans	2 cups	1 cup	1/2 cup
Pepper	1/2 teaspoon	1/4 teaspoon	1/8 teaspoon
Salt (optional)	1/2 teaspoon	1/4 teaspoon	1/8 teaspoon
Water	8 cups	4 cups	2 cups
Canola oil	4 teaspoons	2 teaspoons	1 teaspoon

Heat the water to boiling, remove from heat, add oil, and stir in mix. Cover with a lid, and let the mixture sit for 30 minutes to allow vegetables to hydrate. Bring mixture back to a boil, then turn down the heat, and cook for 30 minutes or until vegetables are tender. Add water if the soup is thicker than desired.

Place water, oil, and mix in slow cooker. Turn on high for the first 30 minutes. Add additional water if needed, then turn down to low, and simmer until ready to eat.

White Bean Chili

Ingredients	6-8 Servings	3-4 Servings	1-2 Servings
Onion	1/4 cup	2 TBS	1 TBS
Corn	1/4 cup	2 TBS	1 TBS
Garlic	4 teaspoons	2 teaspoons	1 teaspoon
Mixed peppers	4 teaspoons	2 teaspoons	1 teaspoon
Oregano	4 teaspoons	2 teaspoons	1 teaspoon
Cumin	4 teaspoons	2 teaspoons	1 teaspoon
TVP chicken bits	1/2 cup	1/4 cup	2 TBS
Tomato dices	1/2 cup	1/4 cup	2 TBS
Tomato powder	1/2 cup	1/4 cup	2 TBS
Sugar	4 teaspoons	2 teaspoons	1 teaspoon
Beef bouillon	4 teaspoons	2 teaspoons	1 teaspoon
Navy beans	1 cup	1/2 cup	1/4 cup
Pepper	1/2 teaspoon	1/4 teaspoon	1/8 teaspoon
Salt (optional)	1/2 teaspoon	1/4 teaspoon	1/8 teaspoon
Water	8 cups	4 cups	2 cups
Canola oil	4 teaspoons	2 teaspoons	1 teaspoon

 Heat the water to boiling, remove from heat, add oil, and stir in mix. Cover with a lid, and let the mixture sit for 30 minutes to allow vegetables to hydrate. Bring mixture back to a boil, then turn down the heat, and cook for 30 minutes or until vegetables are tender. Add water if the soup is thicker than desired.

Place water, oil, and mix in slow cooker. Turn on high for the first 30 minutes. Add additional water if needed, then turn down to low, and simmer until ready to eat.

Quinoa and Black Bean Chili

Ingredients	6-8 Servings	3-4 Servings	1-2 Servings
Chicken bouillon	4 teaspoons	2 teaspoons	1 teaspoon
Onion	4 teaspoons	2 teaspoons	1 teaspoon
Garlic	2 teaspoons	1 teaspoon	1/2 teaspoon
Chili powder	4 teaspoons	2 teaspoons	1 teaspoon
Cumin	4 teaspoons	2 teaspoons	1 teaspoon
Tomato dices	4 teaspoons	2 teaspoons	1 teaspoon
Tomato powder	4 teaspoons	2 teaspoons	1 teaspoon
Sugar	2 teaspoons	1 teaspoon	1/2 teaspoon
Vinegar powder	1 teaspoon	1/2 teaspoon	1/4 teaspoon
Mixed peppers	2 teaspoons	1 teaspoon	1/2 teaspoon
Zucchini	2 teaspoons	1 teaspoon	1/2 teaspoon
Jalapeño	1 teaspoon	1/2 teaspoon	1/4 teaspoon
Red pepper flakes	1 teaspoon	1/2 teaspoon	1/4 teaspoon
Oregano	4 teaspoons	2 teaspoons	1 teaspoon
Cilantro	4 teaspoons	2 teaspoons	1 teaspoon
Black Beans	1/2 cup	1/4 cup	2 TBS
Quinoa	1/2 cup	1/4 cup	2 TBS
Potato dices	1/2 cup	1/4 cup	2 TBS
Corn	1/4 cup	2 TBS	1 TBS
Pepper	1/2 teaspoon	1/4 teaspoon	1/8 teaspoon
Salt (optional)	1/2 teaspoon	1/4 teaspoon	1/8 teaspoon
Water	8 cups	4 cups	2 cups
Olive Oil	4 teaspoons	2 teaspoons	1 teaspoon

Heat the water to boiling, remove from heat, add oil, and stir in mix. Cover with a lid, and let the mixture sit for 30 minutes to allow vegetables to hydrate. Bring mixture back to a boil, then turn down the heat, and cook for 30 minutes or until vegetables are tender. Add water if the soup is thicker than desired.

Place water, oil, and mix in slow cooker. Turn on high for the first 30 minutes. Add additional water if needed, then turn down to low, and simmer until ready to eat.

Hearty Vegetable Bean Chili

Ingredients	6-8 Servings	3-4 Servings	1-2 Servings
Onion	4 teaspoons	2 teaspoons	1 teaspoon
Garlic	4 teaspoons	2 teaspoons	1 teaspoon
Chili powder	4 teaspoons	2 teaspoons	1 teaspoon
Cumin	2 teaspoons	1 teaspoon	1/2 teaspoon
Parsley	4 teaspoons	2 teaspoons	1 teaspoon
Tomato dices	4 teaspoons	2 teaspoons	1 teaspoon
Tomato powder	1/4 cup	2 TBS	1 TBS
Sugar	2 teaspoons	1 teaspoon	1/2 teaspoon
Red wine powder	4 teaspoons	2 teaspoons	1 teaspoon
Mixed peppers	2 teaspoons	1 teaspoon	1/2 teaspoon
Zucchini	4 teaspoons	2 teaspoons	1 teaspoon
Spinach	4 teaspoons	2 teaspoons	1 teaspoon
Jalapeño	1 teaspoon	1/2 teaspoon	1/4 teaspoon
Red pepper flakes	1 teaspoon	1/2 teaspoon	1/4 teaspoon
Oregano	2 teaspoons	1 teaspoon	1/2 teaspoon
Cilantro	2 teaspoons	1 teaspoon	1/2 teaspoon
Black beans	1/4 cup	2 TBS	1 TBS
Garbanzo beans	1/4 cup	2 TBS	1 TBS
Kidney beans	1/4 cup	2 TBS	1 TBS
Corn	1/4 cup	2 TBS	1 TBS
Pepper	1/2 teaspoon	1/4 teaspoon	1/8 teaspoon
Salt (optional)	1/2 teaspoon	1/4 teaspoon	1/8 teaspoon
Water	8 cups	4 cups	2 cups
Olive oil	4 teaspoons	2 teaspoons	1 teaspoon

Heat the water to boiling, remove from heat, add oil, and stir in mix. Cover with a lid, and let the mixture sit for 30 minutes to allow vegetables to hydrate. Bring mixture back to a boil, then turn down the heat, and cook for 30 minutes or until vegetables are tender. Add water if the soup is thicker than desired.

Place water, oil, and mix in slow cooker. Turn on high for the first 30 minutes. Add additional water if needed, then turn down to low, and simmer until ready to eat.

TVP Chicken White Chili

Ingredients	6-8 Servings	3-4 Servings	1-2 Servings
Northern beans	1 cup	1/2 cup	1/4 cup
TVP chicken bits	1 cup	1/2 cup	1/4 cup
Garlic	4 teaspoons	2 teaspoons	1 teaspoon
Onion	1/3 cup	8 teaspoons	4 teaspoons
Ginger	2 teaspoons	1 teaspoon	1/2 teaspoon
Sage	2 teaspoons	1 teaspoon	1/2 teaspoon
Cumin	2 teaspoons	1 teaspoon	1/2 teaspoon
Butter powder	4 teaspoons	2 teaspoons	1 teaspoon
All purpose flour	1/4 cup	2 TBS	1 TBS
Chicken bouillon	4 teaspoons	2 teaspoons	1 teaspoon
Pepper	1/2 teaspoon	1/4 teaspoon	1/8 teaspoon
Salt (optional)	1/2 teaspoon	1/4 teaspoon	1/8 teaspoon
Water	8 cups	4 cups	2 cups
Olive oil	4 teaspoons	2 teaspoons	1 teaspoon

Heat the water to boiling, remove from heat, add oil, and stir in mix. Cover with a lid, and let the mixture sit for 30 minutes to allow vegetables to hydrate. Bring mixture back to a boil, then turn down the heat, and cook for 30 minutes or until vegetables are tender. Add water if the soup is thicker than desired.

Place water, oil, and mix in slow cooker. Turn on high for the first 30 minutes. Add additional water if needed, then turn down to low, and simmer until ready to eat.

TVP Beefy Chili

Ingredients	6-8 Servings	3-4 Servings	1-2 Servings
Kidney beans	1 cup	1/2 cup	1/4 cup
TVP beef bits	1 cup	1/2 cup	1/4 cup
Mixed peppers	1 teaspoon	1/2 teaspoon	1/4 teaspoon
Garlic	4 teaspoons	2 teaspoons	1 teaspoon
Onion	1/3 cup	8 teaspoons	4 teaspoons
Parsley	2 teaspoons	1 teaspoon	1/2 teaspoon
Jalapeño	1 teaspoon	1/2 teaspoon	1/4 teaspoon
Cumin	1 teaspoon	1/2 teaspoon	1/4 teaspoon
Red wine powder	1/4 cup	2 TBS	1 TBS
Tomato dices	1/4 cup	2 TBS	1 TBS
Tomato powder	1/4 cup	2 TBS	1 TBS
Sugar	2 teaspoons	1 teaspoon	1/2 teaspoon
Vinegar powder	2 teaspoons	1 teaspoon	1/2 teaspoon
Beef bouillon	4 teaspoons	2 teaspoons	1 teaspoon
Pepper	1/2 teaspoon	1/4 teaspoon	1/8 teaspoon
Salt (optional)	1/2 teaspoon	1/4 teaspoon	1/8 teaspoon
Water	8 cups	4 cups	2 cups
Olive oil	4 teaspoons	2 teaspoons	1 teaspoon

 Heat the water to boiling, remove from heat, add oil, and stir in mix. Cover with a lid, and let the mixture sit for 30 minutes to allow vegetables to hydrate. Bring mixture back to a boil, then turn down the heat, and cook for 30 minutes or until vegetables are tender. Add water if the soup is thicker than desired.

Place water, oil, and mix in slow cooker. Turn on high for the first 30 minutes. Add additional water if needed, then turn down to low, and simmer until ready to eat.

Italian Chili

Ingredients	6-8 Servings	3-4 Servings	1-2 Servings
TVP beef bits	3/4 cup	6 TBS	3 TBS
Kidney beans	1 cup	1/2 cup	1/4 cup
Chili powder	4 teaspoons	2 teaspoons	1 teaspoon
Garlic	4 teaspoons	2 teaspoons	1 teaspoon
Onion	1/4 cup	2 TBS	1 TBS
Cocoa	2 teaspoons	1 teaspoon	1/2 teaspoon
Worcestershire powder	2 teaspoons	1 teaspoon	1/2 teaspoon
Cumin	2 teaspoons	1 teaspoon	1/2 teaspoon
Allspice	2 teaspoons	1 teaspoon	1/2 teaspoon
Cinnamon	2 teaspoons	1 teaspoon	1/2 teaspoon
Cayenne pepper	1/2 teaspoon	1/4 teaspoon	1/8 teaspoon
Cloves	1/2 teaspoon	1/4 teaspoon	1/8 teaspoon
Tomato dices	1/4 cup	2 TBS	1 TBS
Tomato powder	1/3 cup	8 teaspoons	4 teaspoons
Sugar	2 teaspoons	1 teaspoon	1/2 teaspoon
Vinegar powder	2 teaspoons	1 teaspoon	1/2 teaspoon
Beef bouillon	4 teaspoons	2 teaspoons	1 teaspoon
Pepper	1/2 teaspoon	1/4 teaspoon	1/8 teaspoon
Salt (optional)	1/2 teaspoon	1/4 teaspoon	1/8 teaspoon
Water	8 cups	4 cups	2 cups
Cooked spaghetti	4 cups	2 cups	1 cup

Heat the water to boiling, remove from heat, and stir in mix. Put a lid on the pot and let the mixture sit for 30 minutes. This will re-hydrate most of the contents. Stir the mixture, and add the oil and additional water if needed before bringing the mixture back to a boil. Turn the heat to simmer and cook for an additional 30 minutes—stirring often. Mix in cooked pasta and serve.

Place water, oil, and mix in slow cooker. Turn on high and cook covered for the first 30 minutes. Add additional water if needed. The mixture should be a thin chili. Turn down to low, and simmer until ready to eat. Mix in cooked pasta and serve.

Hearty Vegan Bean Chili

Ingredients	6-8 Servings	3-4 Servings	1-2 Servings
Onion	4 teaspoons	2 teaspoons	1 teaspoon
Garlic	2 teaspoons	1 teaspoon	1/2 teaspoon
Ranch dressing mix	2 teaspoons	1 teaspoon	1/2 teaspoon
TVP taco bits	1 cup	1/2 cup	1/4 cup
Tomato dices	4 teaspoons	2 teaspoons	1 teaspoon
Tomato powder	1/4 cup	2 TBS	1 TBS
Sugar	2 teaspoons	1 teaspoon	1/2 teaspoon
Red wine powder	4 teaspoons	2 teaspoons	1 teaspoon
Jalapeño	1 teaspoon	1/2 teaspoon	1/4 teaspoon
Red pepper flakes	1 teaspoon	1/2 teaspoon	1/4 teaspoon
Black beans	1/4 cup	2 TBS	1 TBS
Pinto beans	1/4 cup	2 TBS	1 TBS
Kidney beans	1/4 cup	2 TBS	1 TBS
Corn	1/4 cup	2 TBS	1 TBS
Pepper	1/2 teaspoon	1/4 teaspoon	1/8 teaspoon
Salt (optional)	1/2 teaspoon	1/4 teaspoon	1/8 teaspoon
Water	8 cups	4 cups	2 cups
Canola oil	4 teaspoons	2 teaspoons	1 teaspoon

Heat the water to boiling, remove from heat, add oil, and stir in mix. Cover with a lid, and let the mixture sit for 30 minutes to allow vegetables to hydrate. Bring mixture back to a boil, then turn down the heat, and cook for 30 minutes or until vegetables are tender. Add water if the soup is thicker than desired.

Place water, oil, and mix in slow cooker. Turn on high for the first 30 minutes. Add additional water if needed, then turn down to low, and simmer until ready to eat.

Spicy Black Bean Chili

Ingredients	6-8 Servings	3-4 Servings	1-2 Servings
Onion	4 teaspoons	2 teaspoons	1 teaspoon
Garlic	2 teaspoons	1 teaspoon	1/2 teaspoon
Mixed peppers	1 teaspoon	1/2 teaspoon	1/4 teaspoon
TVP beef bits	3/4 cup	6 TBS	3 TBS
Tomato dices	4 teaspoons	2 teaspoons	1 teaspoon
Tomato powder	1/4 cup	2 TBS	1 TBS
Sugar	2 teaspoons	1 teaspoon	1/2 teaspoon
Red wine powder	4 teaspoons	2 teaspoons	1 teaspoon
Chili powder	4 teaspoons	2 teaspoons	1 teaspoon
Cumin	2 teaspoons	1 teaspoon	1/2 teaspoon
Italian seasoning	1 teaspoon	1/2 teaspoon	1/4 teaspoon
Red pepper flakes	1 teaspoon	1/2 teaspoon	1/4 teaspoon
Black beans	1 cup	1/2 cup	1/4 cup
Chicken bouillon	2 teaspoons	1 teaspoon	1/2 teaspoon
Pepper	1/2 teaspoon	1/4 teaspoon	1/8 teaspoon
Salt (optional)	1/2 teaspoon	1/4 teaspoon	1/8 teaspoon
Water	8 cups	4 cups	2 cups
Olive oil	4 teaspoons	2 teaspoons	1 teaspoon

Heat the water to boiling, remove from heat, add oil, and stir in mix. Cover with a lid, and let the mixture sit for 30 minutes to allow vegetables to hydrate. Bring mixture back to a boil, then turn down the heat, and cook for 30 minutes or until vegetables are tender. Add water if the soup is thicker than desired.

Place water, oil, and mix in slow cooker. Turn on high for the first 30 minutes. Add additional water if needed, then turn down to low, and simmer until ready to eat.

Pinto Bean Chili

Ingredients	6-8 Servings	3-4 Servings	1-2 Servings
Onion	4 teaspoons	2 teaspoons	1 teaspoon
Garlic	2 teaspoons	1 teaspoon	1/2 teaspoon
Paprika	2 teaspoons	1 teaspoon	1/2 teaspoon
Mixed peppers	1 teaspoon	1/2 teaspoon	1/4 teaspoon
TVP beef bits	3/4 cup	6 TBS	3 TBS
Tomato powder	3/4 cup	6 TBS	3 TBS
Sugar	2 teaspoons	1 teaspoon	1/2 teaspoon
Vinegar powder	2 teaspoons	1 teaspoon	1/2 teaspoon
Chili powder	4 teaspoons	2 teaspoons	1 teaspoon
Cumin	4 teaspoons	2 teaspoons	1 teaspoon
Cocoa, unsweetened	4 teaspoons	2 teaspoons	1 teaspoon
Red pepper flakes	1 teaspoon	1/2 teaspoon	1/4 teaspoon
Pinto beans	1 cup	1/2 cup	1/4 cup
Chicken bouillon	2 teaspoons	1 teaspoon	1/2 teaspoon
Pepper	1/2 teaspoon	1/4 teaspoon	1/8 teaspoon
Salt (optional)	1/2 teaspoon	1/4 teaspoon	1/8 teaspoon
Water	8 cups	4 cups	2 cups
Olive oil	4 teaspoons	2 teaspoons	1 teaspoon

 Heat the water to boiling, remove from heat, add oil, and stir in mix. Cover with a lid, and let the mixture sit for 30 minutes to allow vegetables to hydrate. Bring mixture back to a boil, then turn down the heat, and cook for 30 minutes or until vegetables are tender. Add water if the soup is thicker than desired.

Place water, oil, and mix in slow cooker. Turn on high for the first 30 minutes. Add additional water if needed, then turn down to low, and simmer until ready to eat.

Southern Chili

Ingredients	6-8 Servings	3-4 Servings	1-2 Servings
Kidney beans	2 cups	1 cup	1/2 cup
TVP beef bits	3/4 cup	6 TBS	3 TBS
Garlic	4 teaspoons	2 teaspoons	1 teaspoon
Onion	2 teaspoons	1 teaspoon	1/2 teaspoon
Mixed peppers	2 teaspoons	1 teaspoon	1/2 teaspoon
Chili powder	4 teaspoons	2 teaspoons	1 teaspoon
Worcestershire powder	1 teaspoon	1/2 teaspoon	1/4 teaspoon
Mustard powder	1/2 teaspoon	1/4 teaspoon	1/8 teaspoon
Tomato dices	1/4 cup	2 TBS	1 TBS
Tomato powder	1/2 cup	1/4 cup	2 TBS
Sugar	4 teaspoons	2 teaspoons	1 teaspoon
Cumin	4 teaspoons	2 teaspoons	1 teaspoon
Beef bouillon	4 teaspoons	2 teaspoons	1 teaspoon
Pepper	1/2 teaspoon	1/4 teaspoon	1/8 teaspoon
Salt (optional)	1/2 teaspoon	1/4 teaspoon	1/8 teaspoon
Water	8 cups	4 cups	2 cups

Heat the water to boiling, remove from heat, and stir in mix. Cover with a lid, and let the mixture sit for 30 minutes to allow vegetables to hydrate. Bring mixture back to a boil, then turn down the heat, and cook for 30 minutes or until vegetables are tender. Add water if the soup is thicker than desired.

Place water and mix in slow cooker. Turn on high for the first 30 minutes. Add additional water if needed, then turn down to low, and simmer until ready to eat.

Corn Chili

Ingredients	6-8 Servings	3-4 Servings	1-2 Servings
Kidney beans	3/4 cup	6 TBS	3 TBS
Corn	3/4 cup	6 TBS	3 TBS
TVP beef bits	3/4 cup	6 TBS	3 TBS
Garlic	4 teaspoons	2 teaspoons	1 teaspoon
Onion	4 teaspoons	2 teaspoons	1 teaspoon
Jalapeño	1 teaspoon	1/2 teaspoon	1/4 teaspoon
Mixed peppers	2 teaspoons	1 teaspoon	1/2 teaspoon
Chili powder	4 teaspoons	2 teaspoons	1 teaspoon
Tomato dices	1/4 cup	2 TBS	1 TBS
Tomato powder	1/2 cup	1/4 cup	2 TBS
Sugar	4 teaspoons	2 teaspoons	1 teaspoon
Pepper	1/2 teaspoon	1/4 teaspoon	1/8 teaspoon
Salt (optional)	1/2 teaspoon	1/4 teaspoon	1/8 teaspoon
Water	8 cups	4 cups	2 cups

Heat the water to boiling, remove from heat, and stir in mix. Cover with a lid, and let the mixture sit for 30 minutes to allow vegetables to hydrate. Bring mixture back to a boil, then turn down the heat, and cook for 30 minutes or until vegetables are tender. Add water if the soup is thicker than desired.

Place water and mix in slow cooker. Turn on high for the first 30 minutes. Add additional water if needed, then turn down to low, and simmer until ready to eat.

Kidney Beans Chili

Ingredients	6-8 Servings	3-4 Servings	1-2 Servings
Kidney beans	1 cup	1/2 cup	1/4 cup
TVP beef bits	3/4 cup	6 TBS	3 TBS
Garlic	4 teaspoons	2 teaspoons	1 teaspoon
Onion	4 teaspoons	2 teaspoons	1 teaspoon
Jalapeño	1 teaspoon	1/2 teaspoon	1/4 teaspoon
Mixed peppers	2 teaspoons	1 teaspoon	1/2 teaspoon
Parsley	2 teaspoons	1 teaspoon	1/2 teaspoon
Paprika	1 teaspoon	1/2 teaspoon	1/4 teaspoon
Chili powder	4 teaspoons	2 teaspoons	1 teaspoon
Tomato dices	1/4 cup	2 TBS	1 TBS
Tomato powder	1/2 cup	1/4 cup	2 TBS
Sugar	4 teaspoons	2 teaspoons	1 teaspoon
Pepper	1/2 teaspoon	1/4 teaspoon	1/8 teaspoon
Salt (optional)	1/2 teaspoon	1/4 teaspoon	1/8 teaspoon
Water	8 cups	4 cups	2 cups
Cooked pasta	4 cups	2 cups	1 cup

 Heat the water to boiling, remove from heat, and stir in mix. Cover with a lid, and let the mixture sit for 30 minutes to allow vegetables to hydrate. Bring mixture back to a boil, then turn down the heat, and cook for 30 minutes or until vegetables are tender. Add water if the soup is thicker than desired. Stir in cooked and drained pasta before serving.

Place water and mix in slow cooker. Turn on high for the first 30 minutes. Add additional water if needed, then turn down to low, and simmer until ready to eat. Stir in cooked and drained pasta before serving.

TVP Beef and Bean Chili

Ingredients	6-8 Servings	3-4 Servings	1-2 Servings
Kidney beans	1 cup	1/2 cup	1/4 cup
TVP beef bits	3/4 cup	6 TBS	3 TBS
Beef bouillon	1 teaspoon	1/2 teaspoon	1/4 teaspoon
Garlic	4 teaspoons	2 teaspoons	1 teaspoon
Onion	2 teaspoons	1 teaspoon	1/2 teaspoon
Jalapeño	1 teaspoon	1/2 teaspoon	1/4 teaspoon
Mixed peppers	2 teaspoons	1 teaspoon	1/2 teaspoon
Oregano	2 teaspoons	1 teaspoon	1/2 teaspoon
Paprika	1 teaspoon	1/2 teaspoon	1/4 teaspoon
Cumin	4 teaspoons	2 teaspoons	1 teaspoon
Cocoa, unsweetened	2 teaspoons	1 teaspoon	1/2 teaspoon
Cornmeal	2 teaspoons	1 teaspoon	1/2 teaspoon
All purpose flour	2 teaspoons	1 teaspoon	1/2 teaspoon
Chili powder	4 teaspoons	2 teaspoons	1 teaspoon
Beef bouillon	4 teaspoons	2 teaspoons	1 teaspoon
Tomato dices	1/4 cup	2 TBS	1 TBS
Tomato powder	1/2 cup	1/4 cup	2 TBS
Vinegar powder	2 teaspoons	1 teaspoon	1/2 teaspoon
Sugar	4 teaspoons	2 teaspoons	1 teaspoon
Pepper	1/2 teaspoon	1/4 teaspoon	1/8 teaspoon
Salt (optional)	1/2 teaspoon	1/4 teaspoon	1/8 teaspoon
Water	8 cups	4 cups	2 cups

Heat the water to boiling, remove from heat, and stir in mix. Cover with a lid, and let the mixture sit for 30 minutes to allow vegetables to hydrate. Bring mixture back to a boil, then turn down the heat, and cook for 30 minutes or until vegetables are tender. Add water if the soup is thicker than desired.

Place water and mix in slow cooker. Turn on high for the first 30 minutes. Add additional water if needed, then turn down to low, and simmer until ready to eat.

Quinoa Soup Mixes

What is Quinoa?

Quinoa (pronounced KEEN WAH) is a South American native food that resembles grits or cream of wheat. Quinoa is wheat-free, gluten-free, grain-complete protein that contains all nine essential amino acids. Quinoa is rich in magnesium, folate, phophorus, and lysine, providing nutritional benefits for persons with migraine headaches, diabetes, and atherosclerosis.

Quinoa has a fluffy, creamy, slightly crunchy texture and a nutty flavor. The grain once considered the "gold of the Incas" is actually a seed that is related to beets, spinach, and Swiss chard. Quinoa in soup adds heartiness and nutrition while absorbing the flavors of the soup.

Quinoa Vegetable Soup

Ingredients	6-8 Servings	3-4 Servings	1-2 Servings
Quinoa	1 cup	1/2 cup	1/4 cup
Celery	4 teaspoons	2 teaspoons	1 teaspoon
Carrots	4 teaspoons	2 teaspoons	1 teaspoon
Chicken bouillon	4 teaspoons	2 teaspoons	1 teaspoon
Garlic	4 teaspoons	2 teaspoons	1 teaspoon
Onion	4 teaspoons	2 teaspoons	1 teaspoon
Mixed peppers	2 teaspoons	1 teaspoon	1/2 teaspoon
Parsley	4 teaspoons	2 teaspoons	1 teaspoon
Cabbage	4 teaspoons	2 teaspoons	1 teaspoon
Tomato dices	1/4 cup	2 TBS	1 TBS
Tomato powder	1/2 cup	1/4 cup	2 TBS
Sugar	2 teaspoons	1 teaspoon	1/2 teaspoon
Vinegar powder	2 teaspoons	1 teaspoon	1/2 teaspoon
Pepper	1/2 teaspoon	1/4 teaspoon	1/8 teaspoon
Salt (optional)	1/2 teaspoon	1/4 teaspoon	1/8 teaspoon
Water	8 cups	4 cups	2 cups
Canola oil	4 teaspoons	2 teaspoons	1 teaspoon

 Heat the water to boiling, remove from heat, add oil, and stir in mix. Cover with a lid, and let the mixture sit for 30 minutes to allow vegetables to hydrate. Bring mixture back to a boil, then turn down the heat, and cook for 30 minutes or until vegetables are tender. Add water if the soup is thicker than desired.

Place water, oil, and mix in slow cooker. Turn on high for the first 30 minutes. Add additional water if needed, then turn down to low, and simmer until ready to eat.

Quinoa Squash Soup

Ingredients	6-8 Servings	3-4 Servings	1-2 Servings
Quinoa	1 cup	1/2 cup	1/4 cup
Sweet potatoes	1/2 cup	1/4 cup	2 TBS
Zucchini	1/4 cup	2 TBS	1 TBS
Chicken bouillon	4 teaspoons	2 teaspoons	1 teaspoon
TVP chicken bits	1/2 cup	1/4 cup	2 TBS
Onion	4 teaspoons	2 teaspoons	1 teaspoon
Cumin	2 teaspoons	1 teaspoon	1/2 teaspoon
Apricot bits	4 teaspoons	2 teaspoons	1 teaspoon
Sugar	4 teaspoons	2 teaspoons	1 teaspoon
Vinegar powder	2 teaspoons	1 teaspoon	1/2 teaspoon
Pepper	1/2 teaspoon	1/4 teaspoon	1/8 teaspoon
Salt (optional)	1/2 teaspoon	1/4 teaspoon	1/8 teaspoon
Water	8 cups	4 cups	2 cups
Canola oil	4 teaspoons	2 teaspoons	1 teaspoon

Heat the water to boiling, remove from heat, add oil, and stir in mix. Cover with a lid, and let the mixture sit for 30 minutes to allow vegetables to hydrate. Bring mixture back to a boil, then turn down the heat, and cook for 30 minutes or until vegetables are tender. Add water if the soup is thicker than desired.

Place water, oil, and mix in slow cooker. Turn on high for the first 30 minutes. Add additional water if needed, then turn down to low, and simmer until ready to eat.

Quinoa Mushroom Soup

Ingredients	6-8 Servings	3-4 Servings	1-2 Servings
Quinoa	1/4 cup	2 TBS	1 TBS
Chicken bouillon	4 teaspoons	2 teaspoons	1 teaspoon
Onion	4 teaspoons	2 teaspoons	1 teaspoon
Chives	2 teaspoons	1 teaspoon	1/2 teaspoon
Molasses powder	4 teaspoons	2 teaspoons	1 teaspoon
Sugar	4 teaspoons	2 teaspoons	1 teaspoon
Mushrooms	1 cup	1/2 cup	1/4 cup
Red wine powder	4 teaspoons	2 teaspoons	1 teaspoon
Dry milk	1/4 cup	2 TBS	1 TBS
Butter powder	4 teaspoons	2 teaspoons	1 teaspoon
Pepper	1/2 teaspoon	1/4 teaspoon	1/8 teaspoon
Salt (optional)	1/2 teaspoon	1/4 teaspoon	1/8 teaspoon
Water	8 cups	4 cups	2 cups
Canola oil	4 teaspoons	2 teaspoons	1 teaspoon

Heat the water to boiling, remove from heat, add oil, and stir in mix. Cover with a lid, and let the mixture sit for 30 minutes to allow vegetables to hydrate. Bring mixture back to a boil, then turn down the heat, and cook for 30 minutes or until vegetables are tender. Add water if the soup is thicker than desired.

Place water, oil, and mix in slow cooker. Turn on high for the first 30 minutes. Add additional water if needed, then turn down to low, and simmer until ready to eat.

Creole Quinoa Soup

Ingredients	6-8 Servings	3-4 Servings	1-2 Servings
Quinoa	1/4 cup	2 TBS	1 TBS
Kidney beans	1/2 cup	1/4 cup	2 TBS
Tomato dices	1/4 cup	2 TBS	1 TBS
Tomato powder	1/2 cup	1/4 cup	2 TBS
Sugar	2 teaspoons	1 teaspoon	1/2 teaspoon
Chicken bouillon	4 teaspoons	2 teaspoons	1 teaspoon
Mixed peppers	8 teaspoons	4 teaspoons	2 teaspoons
Onion	4 teaspoons	2 teaspoons	1 teaspoon
Garlic	4 teaspoons	2 teaspoons	1 teaspoon
Cajun seasoning	4 teaspoons	2 teaspoons	1 teaspoon
Cilantro	1 teaspoon	1/2 teaspoon	1/4 teaspoon
Pepper	1/2 teaspoon	1/4 teaspoon	1/8 teaspoon
Salt (optional)	1/2 teaspoon	1/4 teaspoon	1/8 teaspoon
Water	8 cups	4 cups	2 cups
Canola oil	4 teaspoons	2 teaspoons	1 teaspoon

Heat the water to boiling, remove from heat, add oil, and stir in mix. Cover with a lid, and let the mixture sit for 30 minutes to allow vegetables to hydrate. Bring mixture back to a boil, then turn down the heat, and cook for 30 minutes or until vegetables are tender. Add water if the soup is thicker than desired.

Place water, oil, and mix in slow cooker. Turn on high for the first 30 minutes. Add additional water if needed, then turn down to low, and simmer until ready to eat.

Quinoa, Kidney Beans, and Corn Soup

Ingredients	6-8 Servings	3-4 Servings	1-2 Servings
Quinoa	1/2 cup	1/4 cup	2 TBS
Kidney beans	1/2 cup	1/4 cup	2 TBS
Corn	1/2 cup	1/4 cup	2 TBS
Mixed peppers	1 teaspoon	1/2 teaspoon	1/4 teaspoon
Chicken bouillon	4 teaspoons	2 teaspoons	1 teaspoon
Garlic	2 teaspoons	1 teaspoon	1/2 teaspoon
Mustard powder	1/2 teaspoon	1/4 teaspoon	1/8 teaspoon
Onion	4 teaspoons	2 teaspoons	1 teaspoon
Cumin	4 teaspoons	2 teaspoons	1 teaspoon
Pepper	1/2 teaspoon	1/4 teaspoon	1/8 teaspoon
Salt (optional)	1/2 teaspoon	1/4 teaspoon	1/8 teaspoon
Water	8 cups	4 cups	2 cups
Canola oil	4 teaspoons	2 teaspoons	1 teaspoon

Heat the water to boiling, remove from heat, add oil, and stir in mix. Cover with a lid, and let the mixture sit for 30 minutes to allow vegetables to hydrate. Bring mixture back to a boil, then turn down the heat, and cook for 30 minutes or until vegetables are tender. Add water if the soup is thicker than desired.

Place water, oil, and mix in slow cooker. Turn on high for the first 30 minutes. Add additional water if needed, then turn down to low, and simmer until ready to eat.

Quinoa Soup

Ingredients	6-8 Servings	3-4 Servings	1-2 Servings
Quinoa	1/4 cup	2 TBS	1 TBS
Sweet potatoes	1/2 cup	1/4 cup	2 TBS
Corn	1/2 cup	1/4 cup	2 TBS
Spinach	1/2 cup	1/4 cup	2 TBS
Sugar	8 teaspoons	4 teaspoons	2 teaspoons
Chicken bouillon	4 teaspoons	2 teaspoons	1 teaspoon
Mixed peppers	2 teaspoons	1 teaspoon	1/2 teaspoon
Onion	4 teaspoons	2 teaspoons	1 teaspoon
Garlic	2 teaspoons	1 teaspoon	1/2 teaspoon
Soy sauce powder	2 teaspoons	1 teaspoon	1/2 teaspoon
Pepper	1/2 teaspoon	1/4 teaspoon	1/8 teaspoon
Salt (optional)	1/2 teaspoon	1/4 teaspoon	1/8 teaspoon
Water	8 cups	4 cups	2 cups
Canola oil	4 teaspoons	2 teaspoons	1 teaspoon

Heat the water to boiling, remove from heat, add oil, and stir in mix. Cover with a lid, and let the mixture sit for 30 minutes to allow vegetables to hydrate. Bring mixture back to a boil, then turn down the heat, and cook for 30 minutes or until vegetables are tender. Add water if the soup is thicker than desired.

Place water, oil, and mix in slow cooker. Turn on high for the first 30 minutes. Add additional water if needed, then turn down to low, and simmer until ready to eat.

Vegetable Quinoa Soup

Ingredients	6-8 Servings	3-4 Servings	1-2 Servings
Quinoa	1 cup	1/2 cup	1/4 cup
Sweet potatoes	1/2 cup	1/4 cup	2 TBS
Mushrooms	1 cup	1/2 cup	1/4 cup
Potato dices	1/2 cup	1/4 cup	2 TBS
Zucchini	4 teaspoons	2 teaspoons	1 teaspoon
Green beans	4 teaspoons	2 teaspoons	1 teaspoon
Tomato powder	1/2 cup	1/4 cup	2 TBS
Sugar	4 teaspoons	2 teaspoons	1 teaspoon
Chicken bouillon	4 teaspoons	2 teaspoons	1 teaspoon
Onion	2 teaspoons	1 teaspoon	1/2 teaspoon
Butter powder	4 teaspoons	2 teaspoons	1 teaspoon
Pepper	1/2 teaspoon	1/4 teaspoon	1/8 teaspoon
Salt (optional)	1/2 teaspoon	1/4 teaspoon	1/8 teaspoon
Water	8 cups	4 cups	2 cups
Canola oil	4 teaspoons	2 teaspoons	1 teaspoon
Parmesan cheese	4 teaspoons	2 teaspoons	1 teaspoon

Heat the water to boiling, remove from heat, add oil, and stir in mix. Cover with a lid, and let the mixture sit for 30 minutes to allow vegetables to hydrate. Bring mixture back to a boil, then turn down the heat, and cook for 30 minutes or until vegetables are tender. Add water if the soup is thicker than desired. Top with parmesan cheese before serving.

Place water, oil, and mix in slow cooker. Turn on high for the first 30 minutes. Add additional water if needed, then turn down to low, and simmer until ready to eat. Top with parmesan cheese before serving.

Creamy Quinoa Vegetable Soup

Ingredients	6-8 Servings	3-4 Servings	1-2 Servings
Quinoa	1/4 cup	2 TBS	1 TBS
Mushrooms	1 cup	1/2 cup	1/4 cup
Green beans	4 teaspoons	2 teaspoons	1 teaspoon
Chicken bouillon	4 teaspoons	2 teaspoons	1 teaspoon
Onion	4 teaspoons	2 teaspoons	1 teaspoon
Tarragon	2 teaspoons	1 teaspoon	1/2 teaspoon
Dry milk	4 teaspoons	2 teaspoons	1 teaspoon
Sour cream powder	1/4 cup	2 TBS	1 TBS
Butter powder	8 teaspoons	4 teaspoons	2 teaspoons
Pepper	1/2 teaspoon	1/4 teaspoon	1/8 teaspoon
Salt (optional)	1/2 teaspoon	1/4 teaspoon	1/8 teaspoon
Water	8 cups	4 cups	2 cups
Canola oil	4 teaspoons	2 teaspoons	1 teaspoon

Heat the water to boiling, remove from heat, add oil, and stir in mix. Cover with a lid, and let the mixture sit for 30 minutes to allow vegetables to hydrate. Bring mixture back to a boil, then turn down the heat, and cook for 30 minutes or until vegetables are tender. Add water if the soup is thicker than desired.

Place water, oil, and mix in slow cooker. Turn on high for the first 30 minutes. Add additional water if needed, then turn down to low, and simmer until ready to eat.

Quinoa Chili

Ingredients	6-8 Servings	3-4 Servings	1-2 Servings
Quinoa	1/4 cup	2 TBS	1 TBS
Zucchini	4 teaspoons	2 teaspoons	1 teaspoon
Corn	1/4 cup	2 TBS	1 TBS
Tomato powder	4 teaspoons	2 teaspoons	1 teaspoon
Sugar	2 teaspoons	1 teaspoon	1/2 teaspoon
Vinegar powder	2 teaspoons	1 teaspoon	1/2 teaspoon
Onion	4 teaspoons	2 teaspoons	1 teaspoon
Garlic	2 teaspoons	1 teaspoon	1/2 teaspoon
Mixed peppers	2 teaspoons	1 teaspoon	1/2 teaspoon
Black beans	1/4 cup	2 TBS	1 TBS
Chili powder	4 teaspoons	2 teaspoons	1 teaspoon
Cumin	2 teaspoons	1 teaspoon	1/2 teaspoon
Oregano	2 teaspoons	1 teaspoon	1/2 teaspoon
Parsley	2 teaspoons	1 teaspoon	1/2 teaspoon
Cilantro	2 teaspoons	1 teaspoon	1/2 teaspoon
Chicken bouillon	4 teaspoons	2 teaspoons	1 teaspoon
TVP beef bits	1 cup	1/2 cup	1/4 cup
Pepper	1/2 teaspoon	1/4 teaspoon	1/8 teaspoon
Salt (optional)	1/2 teaspoon	1/4 teaspoon	1/8 teaspoon
Water	8 cups	4 cups	2 cups
Canola oil	4 teaspoons	2 teaspoons	1 teaspoon

Heat the water to boiling, remove from heat, add oil, and stir in mix. Cover with a lid, and let the mixture sit for 30 minutes to allow vegetables to hydrate. Bring mixture back to a boil, then turn down the heat, and cook for 30 minutes or until vegetables are tender. Add water if the soup is thicker than desired.

Place water, oil, and mix in slow cooker. Turn on high for the first 30 minutes. Add additional water if needed, then turn down to low, and simmer until ready to eat.

Curry Quinoa Soup

Ingredients	6-8 Servings	3-4 Servings	1-2 Servings
Quinoa	1/4 cup	2 TBS	1 TBS
TVP chicken bits	1 cup	1/2 cup	1/4 cup
Mushrooms	1 cup	1/2 cup	1/4 cup
Celery	4 teaspoons	2 teaspoons	1 teaspoon
Apple dices	1/2 cup	1/4 cup	2 TBS
Chicken bouillon	4 teaspoons	2 teaspoons	1 teaspoon
Onion	4 teaspoons	2 teaspoons	1 teaspoon
Dry milk	4 teaspoons	2 teaspoons	1 teaspoon
Curry powder	4 teaspoons	2 teaspoons	1 teaspoon
Paprika	1 teaspoon	1/2 teaspoon	1/4 teaspoon
Pepper	1/2 teaspoon	1/4 teaspoon	1/8 teaspoon
Salt (optional)	1/2 teaspoon	1/4 teaspoon	1/8 teaspoon
Water	8 cups	4 cups	2 cups
Canola oil	4 teaspoons	2 teaspoons	1 teaspoon

Heat the water to boiling, remove from heat, add oil, and stir in mix. Cover with a lid, and let the mixture sit for 30 minutes to allow vegetables to hydrate. Bring mixture back to a boil, then turn down the heat, and cook for 30 minutes or until vegetables are tender. Add water if the soup is thicker than desired.

Place water, oil, and mix in slow cooker. Turn on high for the first 30 minutes. Add additional water if needed, then turn down to low, and simmer until ready to eat.

Latin Quinoa Vegetable Soup

Ingredients	6-8 Servings	3-4 Servings	1-2 Servings
Quinoa	1/2 cup	1/4 cup	2 TBS
Zucchini	4 teaspoons	2 teaspoons	1 teaspoon
Potato dices	1/4 cup	2 TBS	1 TBS
Tomato powder	1/4 cup	2 TBS	1 TBS
Tomato dices	4 teaspoons	2 teaspoons	1 teaspoon
Sugar	2 teaspoons	1 teaspoon	1/2 teaspoon
Onion	4 teaspoons	2 teaspoons	1 teaspoon
Garlic	2 teaspoons	1 teaspoon	1/2 teaspoon
Mixed peppers	2 teaspoons	1 teaspoon	1/2 teaspoon
Cumin	2 teaspoons	1 teaspoon	1/2 teaspoon
Oregano	2 teaspoons	1 teaspoon	1/2 teaspoon
Coriander	2 teaspoons	1 teaspoon	1/2 teaspoon
Lime juice powder	2 teaspoons	1 teaspoon	1/2 teaspoon
Chicken bouillon	4 teaspoons	2 teaspoons	1 teaspoon
Pepper	1/2 teaspoon	1/4 teaspoon	1/8 teaspoon
Salt (optional)	1/2 teaspoon	1/4 teaspoon	1/8 teaspoon
Water	8 cups	4 cups	2 cups
Canola oil	4 teaspoons	2 teaspoons	1 teaspoon

Heat the water to boiling, remove from heat, add oil, and stir in mix. Cover with a lid, and let the mixture sit for 30 minutes to allow vegetables to hydrate. Bring mixture back to a boil, then turn down the heat, and cook for 30 minutes or until vegetables are tender. Add water if the soup is thicker than desired.

Place water, oil, and mix in slow cooker. Turn on high for the first 30 minutes. Add additional water if needed, then turn down to low, and simmer until ready to eat.

Quinoa and Kidney Beans Soup

Ingredients	6-8 Servings	3-4 Servings	1-2 Servings
Quinoa	1/2 cup	1/4 cup	2 TBS
Kidney beans	3/4 cup	6 TBS	3 TBS
Mushrooms	1/2 cup	1/4 cup	2 TBS
Spinach	1/4 cup	2 TBS	1 TBS
Chicken bouillon	4 teaspoons	2 teaspoons	1 teaspoon
Onion	4 teaspoons	2 teaspoons	1 teaspoon
Carrots	2 teaspoons	1 teaspoon	1/2 teaspoon
Garlic	2 teaspoons	1 teaspoon	1/2 teaspoon
Cumin	2 teaspoons	1 teaspoon	1/2 teaspoon
Coriander	2 teaspoons	1 teaspoon	1/2 teaspoon
Pepper	1/2 teaspoon	1/4 teaspoon	1/8 teaspoon
Salt (optional)	1/2 teaspoon	1/4 teaspoon	1/8 teaspoon
Water	8 cups	4 cups	2 cups
Canola oil	4 teaspoons	2 teaspoons	1 teaspoon

 Heat the water to boiling, remove from heat, add oil, and stir in mix. Cover with a lid, and let the mixture sit for 30 minutes to allow vegetables to hydrate. Bring mixture back to a boil, then turn down the heat, and cook for 30 minutes or until vegetables are tender. Add water if the soup is thicker than desired.

Place water, oil, and mix in slow cooker. Turn on high for the first 30 minutes. Add additional water if needed, then turn down to low, and simmer until ready to eat.

TVP Chicken Quinoa Soup

Ingredients	6-8 Servings	3-4 Servings	1-2 Servings
Quinoa	1/4 cup	2 TBS	1 TBS
TVP chicken bits	1 cup	1/2 cup	1/4 cup
Chicken bouillon	4 teaspoons	2 teaspoons	1 teaspoon
Butter powder	1/4 cup	2 TBS	1 TBS
Celery	4 teaspoons	2 teaspoons	1 teaspoon
Spinach	4 teaspoons	2 teaspoons	1 teaspoon
Chives	4 teaspoons	2 teaspoons	1 teaspoon
Onion	1/4 cup	2 TBS	1 TBS
Thyme	1 teaspoon	1/2 teaspoon	1/4 teaspoon
Garlic	2 teaspoons	1 teaspoon	1/2 teaspoon
Cumin	2 teaspoons	1 teaspoon	1/2 teaspoon
Parsley	2 teaspoons	1 teaspoon	1/2 teaspoon
Cilantro	1 teaspoon	1/2 teaspoon	1/4 teaspoon
Pepper	1/2 teaspoon	1/4 teaspoon	1/8 teaspoon
Salt (optional)	1/2 teaspoon	1/4 teaspoon	1/8 teaspoon
Water	8 cups	4 cups	2 cups
Canola oil	4 teaspoons	2 teaspoons	1 teaspoon

Heat the water to boiling, remove from heat, add oil, and stir in mix. Cover with a lid, and let the mixture sit for 30 minutes to allow vegetables to hydrate. Bring mixture back to a boil, then turn down the heat, and cook for 30 minutes or until vegetables are tender. Add water if the soup is thicker than desired.

Place water, oil, and mix in slow cooker. Turn on high for the first 30 minutes. Add additional water if needed, then turn down to low, and simmer until ready to eat.

Sweet Potatoes and Quinoa Soup

Ingredients	6-8 Servings	3-4 Servings	1-2 Servings
Quinoa	1 cup	1/2 cup	1/4 cup
Sweet potatoes	1 cup	1/2 cup	1/4 cup
Chicken bouillon	4 teaspoons	2 teaspoons	1 teaspoon
Peanut Butter powder	4 teaspoons	2 teaspoons	1 teaspoon
Corn	1/4 cup	2 TBS	1 TBS
Mixed peppers	2 teaspoons	1 teaspoon	1/2 teaspoon
Onion	1/4 cup	2 TBS	1 TBS
Garlic	2 teaspoons	1 teaspoon	1/2 teaspoon
Cumin	2 teaspoons	1 teaspoon	1/2 teaspoon
Cilantro	1 teaspoon	1/2 teaspoon	1/4 teaspoon
Pepper	1/2 teaspoon	1/4 teaspoon	1/8 teaspoon
Salt (optional)	1/2 teaspoon	1/4 teaspoon	1/8 teaspoon
Water	8 cups	4 cups	2 cups
Canola oil	4 teaspoons	2 teaspoons	1 teaspoon

 Heat the water to boiling, remove from heat, add oil, and stir in mix. Cover with a lid, and let the mixture sit for 30 minutes to allow vegetables to hydrate. Bring mixture back to a boil, then turn down the heat, and cook for 30 minutes or until vegetables are tender. Add water if the soup is thicker than desired.

Place water, oil, and mix in slow cooker. Turn on high for the first 30 minutes. Add additional water if needed, then turn down to low, and simmer until ready to eat.

Carrots, Spinach, and Quinoa Soup

Ingredients	6-8 Servings	3-4 Servings	1-2 Servings
Quinoa	1/4 cup	2 TBS	1 TBS
Chicken bouillon	4 teaspoons	2 teaspoons	1 teaspoon
Spinach	1/2 cup	1/4 cup	2 TBS
Onion	8 teaspoons	4 teaspoons	2 teaspoons
Garlic	4 teaspoons	2 teaspoons	1 teaspoon
Carrots	4 teaspoons	2 teaspoons	1 teaspoon
Cumin	2 teaspoons	1 teaspoon	1/2 teaspoon
Paprika	2 teaspoons	1 teaspoon	1/2 teaspoon
Coriander	1/2 teaspoon	1/4 teaspoon	1/8 teaspoon
Ginger	2 teaspoons	1 teaspoon	1/2 teaspoon
Pepper	1/2 teaspoon	1/4 teaspoon	1/8 teaspoon
Salt (optional)	1/2 teaspoon	1/4 teaspoon	1/8 teaspoon
Water	8 cups	4 cups	2 cups
Canola oil	4 teaspoons	2 teaspoons	1 teaspoon

Heat the water to boiling, remove from heat, add oil, and stir in mix. Cover with a lid, and let the mixture sit for 30 minutes to allow vegetables to hydrate. Bring mixture back to a boil, then turn down the heat, and cook for 30 minutes or until vegetables are tender. Add water if the soup is thicker than desired.

Place water, oil, and mix in slow cooker. Turn on high for the first 30 minutes. Add additional water if needed, then turn down to low, and simmer until ready to eat.

Garbanzo and Quinoa Soup

Ingredients	6-8 Servings	3-4 Servings	1-2 Servings
Quinoa	1/4 cup	2 TBS	1 TBS
Chicken bouillon	4 teaspoons	2 teaspoons	1 teaspoon
TVP chicken bits	1/2 cup	1/4 cup	2 TBS
Zucchini	4 teaspoons	2 teaspoons	1 teaspoon
Garbanzo beans	1/2 cup	1/4 cup	2 TBS
Corn	1/2 cup	1/4 cup	2 TBS
Onion	4 teaspoons	2 teaspoons	1 teaspoon
Mixed peppers	2 teaspoons	1 teaspoon	1/2 teaspoon
Tomato powder	4 teaspoons	2 teaspoons	1 teaspoon
Tomato dices	4 teaspoons	2 teaspoons	1 teaspoon
Sugar	2 teaspoons	1 teaspoon	1/2 teaspoon
Vinegar powder	1 teaspoon	1/2 teaspoon	1/4 teaspoon
Orange juice powder	4 teaspoons	2 teaspoons	1 teaspoon
Cilantro	1 teaspoon	1/2 teaspoon	1/4 teaspoon
Cayenne pepper	1/2 teaspoon	1/4 teaspoon	1/8 teaspoon
Pepper	1/2 teaspoon	1/4 teaspoon	1/8 teaspoon
Salt (optional)	1/2 teaspoon	1/4 teaspoon	1/8 teaspoon
Water	8 cups	4 cups	2 cups
Canola oil	4 teaspoons	2 teaspoons	1 teaspoon

Heat the water to boiling, remove from heat, add oil, and stir in mix. Cover with a lid, and let the mixture sit for 30 minutes to allow vegetables to hydrate. Bring mixture back to a boil, then turn down the heat, and cook for 30 minutes or until vegetables are tender. Add water if the soup is thicker than desired.

Place water, oil, and mix in slow cooker. Turn on high for the first 30 minutes. Add additional water if needed, then turn down to low, and simmer until ready to eat.

African Quinoa Vegetable Soup

Ingredients	6-8 Servings	3-4 Servings	1-2 Servings
Quinoa	1 cup	1/2 cup	1/4 cup
Butter powder	1/4 cup	2 TBS	1 TBS
Onion	4 teaspoons	2 teaspoons	1 teaspoon
Garlic	4 teaspoons	2 teaspoons	1 teaspoon
Jalapeño	2 teaspoons	1 teaspoon	1/2 teaspoon
Mixed peppers	2 teaspoons	1 teaspoon	1/2 teaspoon
Celery	2 teaspoons	1 teaspoon	1/2 teaspoon
Zucchini	4 teaspoons	2 teaspoons	1 teaspoon
Sweet potatoes	1/2 cup	1/4 cup	2 TBS
Cumin	4 teaspoons	2 teaspoons	1 teaspoon
Oregano	2 teaspoons	1 teaspoon	1/2 teaspoon
Peanut Butter powder	1/4 cup	2 TBS	1 TBS
Sugar	1/4 cup	2 TBS	1 TBS
Curry powder powder	4 teaspoons	2 teaspoons	1 teaspoon
Cayenne pepper	1/2 teaspoon	1/4 teaspoon	1/8 teaspoon
Pepper	1/2 teaspoon	1/4 teaspoon	1/8 teaspoon
Salt (optional)	1/2 teaspoon	1/4 teaspoon	1/8 teaspoon
Water	8 cups	4 cups	2 cups
Canola oil	4 teaspoons	2 teaspoons	1 teaspoon

Heat the water to boiling, remove from heat, add oil, and stir in mix. Cover with a lid, and let the mixture sit for 30 minutes to allow vegetables to hydrate. Bring mixture back to a boil, then turn down the heat, and cook for 30 minutes or until vegetables are tender. Add water if the soup is thicker than desired.

Place water, oil, and mix in slow cooker. Turn on high for the first 30 minutes. Add additional water if needed, then turn down to low, and simmer until ready to eat.

Split Pea and Quinoa Soup

Ingredients	6-8 Servings	3-4 Servings	1-2 Servings
Quinoa	1/4 cup	2 TBS	1 TBS
Chicken bouillon	4 teaspoons	2 teaspoons	1 teaspoon
TVP ham bits	1 cup	1/2 cup	1/4 cup
Split peas	1 cup	1/2 cup	1/4 cup
Onion	1/4 cup	2 TBS	1 TBS
Carrots	4 teaspoons	2 teaspoons	1 teaspoon
Pepper	1/2 teaspoon	1/4 teaspoon	1/8 teaspoon
Salt (optional)	1/2 teaspoon	1/4 teaspoon	1/8 teaspoon
Water	8 cups	4 cups	2 cups
Canola oil	4 teaspoons	2 teaspoons	1 teaspoon

Heat the water to boiling, remove from heat, add oil, and stir in mix. Cover with a lid, and let the mixture sit for 30 minutes to allow vegetables to hydrate. Bring mixture back to a boil, then turn down the heat, and cook for 30 minutes or until vegetables are tender. Add water if the soup is thicker than desired.

Place water, oil, and mix in slow cooker. Turn on high for the first 30 minutes. Add additional water if needed, then turn down to low, and simmer until ready to eat.

Curried Garbanzo, Lentil, and Quinoa Soup

Ingredients	6-8 Servings	3-4 Servings	1-2 Servings
Quinoa	1/2 cup	1/4 cup	2 TBS
Chicken bouillon	4 teaspoons	2 teaspoons	1 teaspoon
Carrots	4 teaspoons	2 teaspoons	1 teaspoon
Garbanzo beans	1/2 cup	1/4 cup	2 TBS
Celery	4 teaspoons	2 teaspoons	1 teaspoon
Onion	4 teaspoons	2 teaspoons	1 teaspoon
Lentils	4 teaspoons	2 teaspoons	1 teaspoon
Tomato powder	4 teaspoons	2 teaspoons	1 teaspoon
Tomato dices	4 teaspoons	2 teaspoons	1 teaspoon
Sugar	2 teaspoons	1 teaspoon	1/2 teaspoon
Vinegar powder	4 teaspoons	2 teaspoons	1 teaspoon
Chili powder	4 teaspoons	2 teaspoons	1 teaspoon
Curry powder	4 teaspoons	2 teaspoons	1 teaspoon
Cilantro	1 teaspoon	1/2 teaspoon	1/4 teaspoon
Cayenne pepper	1/2 teaspoon	1/4 teaspoon	1/8 teaspoon
Pepper	1/2 teaspoon	1/4 teaspoon	1/8 teaspoon
Salt (optional)	1/2 teaspoon	1/4 teaspoon	1/8 teaspoon
Water	8 cups	4 cups	2 cups
Canola oil	4 teaspoons	2 teaspoons	1 teaspoon

Heat the water to boiling, remove from heat, add oil, and stir in mix. Cover with a lid, and let the mixture sit for 30 minutes to allow vegetables to hydrate. Bring mixture back to a boil, then turn down the heat, and cook for 30 minutes or until vegetables are tender. Add water if the soup is thicker than desired.

Place water, oil, and mix in slow cooker. Turn on high for the first 30 minutes. Add additional water if needed, then turn down to low, and simmer until ready to eat.

Peruvian Quinoa Soup

Ingredients	6-8 Servings	3-4 Servings	1-2 Servings
Quinoa	1 cup	1/2 cup	1/4 cup
Chicken bouillon	4 teaspoons	2 teaspoons	1 teaspoon
TVP chicken bits	1/2 cup	1/4 cup	2 TBS
Onion	8 teaspoons	4 teaspoons	2 teaspoons
Celery	4 teaspoons	2 teaspoons	1 teaspoon
Potato dices	1/2 cup	1/4 cup	2 TBS
Pepper	1/2 teaspoon	1/4 teaspoon	1/8 teaspoon
Salt (optional)	1/2 teaspoon	1/4 teaspoon	1/8 teaspoon
Water	8 cups	4 cups	2 cups
Canola oil	4 teaspoons	2 teaspoons	1 teaspoon

Heat the water to boiling, remove from heat, add oil, and stir in mix. Cover with a lid, and let the mixture sit for 30 minutes to allow vegetables to hydrate. Bring mixture back to a boil, then turn down the heat, and cook for 30 minutes or until vegetables are tender. Add water if the soup is thicker than desired.

Place water, oil, and mix in slow cooker. Turn on high for the first 30 minutes. Add additional water if needed, then turn down to low, and simmer until ready to eat.

Quinoa Broccoli Soup

Ingredients	6-8 Servings	3-4 Servings	1-2 Servings
Quinoa	1/4 cup	2 TBS	1 TBS
Chicken bouillon	4 teaspoons	2 teaspoons	1 teaspoon
TVP chicken bits	1/2 cup	1/4 cup	2 TBS
Onion	4 teaspoons	2 teaspoons	1 teaspoon
Garlic	4 teaspoons	2 teaspoons	1 teaspoon
Carrots	2 teaspoons	1 teaspoon	1/2 teaspoon
Broccoli	1 cup	1/2 cup	1/4 cup
Pepper	1/2 teaspoon	1/4 teaspoon	1/8 teaspoon
Salt (optional)	1/2 teaspoon	1/4 teaspoon	1/8 teaspoon
Water	8 cups	4 cups	2 cups
Canola oil	4 teaspoons	2 teaspoons	1 teaspoon

 Heat the water to boiling, remove from heat, add oil, and stir in mix. Cover with a lid, and let the mixture sit for 30 minutes to allow vegetables to hydrate. Bring mixture back to a boil, then turn down the heat, and cook for 30 minutes or until vegetables are tender. Add water if the soup is thicker than desired.

Place water, oil, and mix in slow cooker. Turn on high for the first 30 minutes. Add additional water if needed, then turn down to low, and simmer until ready to eat.

Black Bean Soup Mixes

114

Using Dehydrated and Freeze-Dried Legumes

The recipes in this and following sections use dehydrated or freeze-dried legumes. Beans, lentils, or split peas that have been dehydrated or freeze-dried are different than the typical dried versions that you find in the grocery store. Dehydrated and freeze-dried legumes do not have to be pre-soaked and cook in approximately 30 minutes.

> VARIATION: The bean, lentil, and split pea mixes may also be packaged using dried beans, lentils, or split peas instead of the dehydrated or freeze-dried versions. However, the dried legumes must be soaked prior to cooking. Package dried beans, lentils, and split peas separately from the rest of the mix.

Legumes are a great source of soluble fiber, a useful source of vegetarian protein and a good source of energy. They are also good sources of phytochemicals and phytoestrogens, bioactive compounds like isoflavones which may protect against breast cancer.

Dry beans are one of the richest plant sources of protein (6-12 percent protein by cooked weight), are high in carbohydrates (especially dietary fiber), and typically low in fat. Legumes are a useful source of folate. Some types contain vitamin A.

Black Beans

All of the soup mixes in this section include black beans. Black beans, commonly referred to as turtle beans, have a shiny, dark, shell-like appearance. Their rich flavor has been compared to that of mushrooms. They have a velvety texture and hold their shape well during cooking.

Black beans originated in parts of Central and South America. They were introduced into Europe in the fiteenth century by Spanish explorers returning from their voyages to the New World and were subsequently spread to Africa and Asia by Spanish and Portuguese traders. Black beans are an important staple in the cuisines of Mexico, Brazil, Cuba, Guatemala, and the Dominican Republic.

Black beans provide an amazing protein-plus-fiber content. A single, one-cup serving provides nearly 15 grams of fiber (well over half of the daily value) and 15 grams of protein (equivalent to the amount in two ounces of a meat like chicken or a fish like salmon). Black beans provide many health benefits, having positive effects on:

- lowering the risk of colon cancer.
- substantially lowering the risk of type 2 diabetes.
- providing protection against cancers and heart disease.
- preventing blood sugar levels from rising too high in people with diabetes.
- supporting cardiovascular health.
- lowering cholesterol.
- promoting intestinal health.

Black Bean and Corn Chowder

Ingredients	6-8 Servings	3-4 Servings	1-2 Servings
Onion	1/4 cup	2 TBS	1 TBS
Garlic	4 teaspoons	2 teaspoons	1 teaspoon
Oregano	2 teaspoons	1 teaspoon	1/2 teaspoon
Corn	3/4 cup	6 TBS	3 TBS
Chicken bouillon	4 teaspoons	2 teaspoons	1 teaspoon
Chili powder	2 teaspoons	1 teaspoon	1/2 teaspoon
TVP ham bits	1 cup	1/2 cup	1/4 cup
Black beans	2 cups	1 cup	1/2 cup
Pepper	1/2 teaspoon	1/4 teaspoon	1/8 teaspoon
Salt (optional)	1/2 teaspoon	1/4 teaspoon	1/8 teaspoon
Water	8 cups	4 cups	2 cups
Canola oil	4 teaspoons	2 teaspoons	1 teaspoon

Heat the water to boiling, remove from heat, add oil, and stir in mix. Cover with a lid, and let the mixture sit for 30 minutes to allow vegetables to hydrate. Bring mixture back to a boil, then turn down the heat, and cook for 30 minutes or until vegetables are tender. Add water if the soup is thicker than desired.

Place water, oil, and mix in slow cooker. Turn on high for the first 30 minutes. Add additional water if needed, then turn down to low, and simmer until ready to eat.

Hearty Black Bean Soup

Ingredients	6-8 Servings	3-4 Servings	1-2 Servings
Onion	1/4 cup	2 TBS	1 TBS
Garlic	4 teaspoons	2 teaspoons	1 teaspoon
Celery	4 teaspoons	2 teaspoons	1 teaspoon
Cumin	2 teaspoons	1 teaspoon	1/2 teaspoon
Oregano	2 teaspoons	1 teaspoon	1/2 teaspoon
Black beans	2 cups	1 cup	1/2 cup
Pepper	1/2 teaspoon	1/4 teaspoon	1/8 teaspoon
Salt (optional)	1/2 teaspoon	1/4 teaspoon	1/8 teaspoon
Water	8 cups	4 cups	2 cups
Canola oil	4 teaspoons	2 teaspoons	1 teaspoon

Heat the water to boiling, remove from heat, add oil, and stir in mix. Cover with a lid, and let the mixture sit for 30 minutes to allow vegetables to hydrate. Bring mixture back to a boil, then turn down the heat, and cook for 30 minutes or until vegetables are tender. Add water if the soup is thicker than desired.

Place water, oil, and mix in slow cooker. Turn on high for the first 30 minutes. Add additional water if needed, then turn down to low, and simmer until ready to eat.

TVP Ham Black Bean Soup

Ingredients	6-8 Servings	3-4 Servings	1-2 Servings
Onion	1/4 cup	2 TBS	1 TBS
Tomato dices	1/4 cup	2 TBS	1 TBS
Tomato powder	1/4 cup	2 TBS	1 TBS
Sugar	4 teaspoons	2 teaspoons	1 teaspoon
Vinegar powder	4 teaspoons	2 teaspoons	1 teaspoon
Chicken bouillon	4 teaspoons	2 teaspoons	1 teaspoon
TVP ham bits	3/4 cup	6 TBS	3 TBS
Black beans	1 cup	1/2 cup	1/4 cup
Pepper	1/2 teaspoon	1/4 teaspoon	1/8 teaspoon
Salt (optional)	1/2 teaspoon	1/4 teaspoon	1/8 teaspoon
Water	8 cups	4 cups	2 cups
Canola oil	4 teaspoons	2 teaspoons	1 teaspoon

Heat the water to boiling, remove from heat, add oil, and stir in mix. Cover with a lid, and let the mixture sit for 30 minutes to allow vegetables to hydrate. Bring mixture back to a boil, then turn down the heat, and cook for 30 minutes or until vegetables are tender. Add water if the soup is thicker than desired.

Place water, oil, and mix in slow cooker. Turn on high for the first 30 minutes. Add additional water if needed, then turn down to low, and simmer until ready to eat.

Black Bean Vegetable Soup

Ingredients	6-8 Servings	3-4 Servings	1-2 Servings
Onion	1/4 cup	2 TBS	1 TBS
Garlic	4 teaspoons	2 teaspoons	1 teaspoon
Carrots	4 teaspoons	2 teaspoons	1 teaspoon
Corn	1/2 cup	1/4 cup	2 TBS
Tomato dices	1/4 cup	2 TBS	1 TBS
Tomato powder	4 teaspoons	2 teaspoons	1 teaspoon
Sugar	2 teaspoons	1 teaspoon	1/2 teaspoon
Cumin	2 teaspoons	1 teaspoon	1/2 teaspoon
Vegetable bouillon	4 teaspoons	2 teaspoons	1 teaspoon
Chili powder	2 teaspoons	1 teaspoon	1/2 teaspoon
Black beans	2 cups	1 cup	1/2 cup
Pepper	1/2 teaspoon	1/4 teaspoon	1/8 teaspoon
Salt (optional)	1/2 teaspoon	1/4 teaspoon	1/8 teaspoon
Water	8 cups	4 cups	2 cups
Canola oil	4 teaspoons	2 teaspoons	1 teaspoon

Heat the water to boiling, remove from heat, add oil, and stir in mix. Cover with a lid, and let the mixture sit for 30 minutes to allow vegetables to hydrate. Bring mixture back to a boil, then turn down the heat, and cook for 30 minutes or until vegetables are tender. Add water if the soup is thicker than desired.

Place water, oil, and mix in slow cooker. Turn on high for the first 30 minutes. Add additional water if needed, then turn down to low, and simmer until ready to eat.

Creamy Black Bean Soup

Ingredients	6-8 Servings	3-4 Servings	1-2 Servings
Onion	1/4 cup	2 TBS	1 TBS
Carrots	4 teaspoons	2 teaspoons	1 teaspoon
Celery	4 teaspoons	2 teaspoons	1 teaspoon
Garlic	4 teaspoons	2 teaspoons	1 teaspoon
Vegetable bouillon	4 teaspoons	2 teaspoons	1 teaspoon
Oregano	2 teaspoons	1 teaspoon	1/2 teaspoon
Cayenne pepper	1/2 teaspoon	1/4 teaspoon	1/8 teaspoon
TVP ham bits	1/3 cup	3 TBS	4 teaspoons
Black beans	2 cups	1 cup	1/2 cup
Pepper	1/2 teaspoon	1/4 teaspoon	1/8 teaspoon
Salt (optional)	1/2 teaspoon	1/4 teaspoon	1/8 teaspoon
Water	8 cups	4 cups	2 cups
Canola oil	4 teaspoons	2 teaspoons	1 teaspoon

 Heat the water to boiling, remove from heat, add oil, and stir in mix. Cover with a lid, and let the mixture sit for 30 minutes to allow vegetables to hydrate. Bring mixture back to a boil, then turn down the heat, and cook for 30 minutes or until vegetables are tender. Add water if the soup is thicker than desired.

 Place water, oil, and mix in slow cooker. Turn on high for the first 30 minutes. Add additional water if needed, then turn down to low, and simmer until ready to eat.

This soup is good as is, or for a creamy consistency, use a traditional or stick blender and blend to a smooth consistency before serving.

Black Bean Soup

Ingredients	6-8 Servings	3-4 Servings	1-2 Servings
Onion	1/4 cup	2 TBS	1 TBS
Celery	4 teaspoons	2 teaspoons	1 teaspoon
Garlic	4 teaspoons	2 teaspoons	1 teaspoon
Chicken bouillon	4 teaspoons	2 teaspoons	1 teaspoon
Mixed peppers	2 teaspoons	1 teaspoon	1/2 teaspoon
Cumin	1/2 teaspoon	1/4 teaspoon	1/8 teaspoon
Lemon juice powder	2 teaspoons	1 teaspoon	1/2 teaspoon
TVP ham bits	1/2 cup	1/4 cup	2 TBS
Black beans	2 cups	1 cup	1/2 cup
Pepper	1/2 teaspoon	1/4 teaspoon	1/8 teaspoon
Salt (optional)	1/2 teaspoon	1/4 teaspoon	1/8 teaspoon
Water	8 cups	4 cups	2 cups
Canola oil	4 teaspoons	2 teaspoons	1 teaspoon

 Heat the water to boiling, remove from heat, add oil, and stir in mix. Cover with a lid, and let the mixture sit for 30 minutes to allow vegetables to hydrate. Bring mixture back to a boil, then turn down the heat, and cook for 30 minutes or until vegetables are tender. Add water if the soup is thicker than desired.

 Place water, oil, and mix in slow cooker. Turn on high for the first 30 minutes. Add additional water if needed, then turn down to low, and simmer until ready to eat.

This soup is good as is, or for a creamy consistency, use a traditional or stick blender and blend to a smooth consistency before serving.

Spicy Black Bean Soup

Ingredients	6-8 Servings	3-4 Servings	1-2 Servings
Onion	1/4 cup	2 TBS	1 TBS
Garlic	4 teaspoons	2 teaspoons	1 teaspoon
Tomato dices	1/3 cup	8 teaspoons	4 teaspoons
Tomato powder	1/3 cup	8 teaspoons	4 teaspoons
Sugar	4 teaspoons	2 teaspoons	1 teaspoon
Chili powder	2 teaspoons	1 teaspoon	1/2 teaspoon
Cumin	2 teaspoons	1 teaspoon	1/2 teaspoon
Lime juice powder	2 teaspoons	1 teaspoon	1/2 teaspoon
TVP taco bits	1/2 cup	1/4 cup	2 TBS
Black beans	2 cups	1 cup	1/2 cup
Pepper	1/2 teaspoon	1/4 teaspoon	1/8 teaspoon
Salt (optional)	1/2 teaspoon	1/4 teaspoon	1/8 teaspoon
Water	8 cups	4 cups	2 cups
Canola oil	4 teaspoons	2 teaspoons	1 teaspoon

 Heat the water to boiling, remove from heat, add oil, and stir in mix. Cover with a lid, and let the mixture sit for 30 minutes to allow vegetables to hydrate. Bring mixture back to a boil, then turn down the heat, and cook for 30 minutes or until vegetables are tender. Add water if the soup is thicker than desired.

 Place water, oil, and mix in slow cooker. Turn on high for the first 30 minutes. Add additional water if needed, then turn down to low, and simmer until ready to eat.

This soup is good as is, or for a creamy consistency, use a traditional or stick blender and blend to a smooth consistency before serving.

Yummy Black Bean Soup

Ingredients	6-8 Servings	3-4 Servings	1-2 Servings
Onion	1/4 cup	2 TBS	1 TBS
Garlic	4 teaspoons	2 teaspoons	1 teaspoon
Thyme	2 teaspoons	1 teaspoon	1/2 teaspoon
Tomato dices	1/4 cup	2 TBS	1 TBS
Tomato powder	1/4 cup	2 TBS	1 TBS
Sugar	2 teaspoons	1 teaspoon	1/2 teaspoon
Butter powder	1/2 cup	1/4 cup	2 TBS
Cumin	2 teaspoons	1 teaspoon	1/2 teaspoon
Cayenne pepper	1 teaspoon	1/2 teaspoon	1/4 teaspoon
TVP beef bits	1/2 cup	1/4 cup	2 TBS
Black beans	2 cups	1 cup	1/2 cup
Pepper	1/2 teaspoon	1/4 teaspoon	1/8 teaspoon
Salt (optional)	1/2 teaspoon	1/4 teaspoon	1/8 teaspoon
Water	8 cups	4 cups	2 cups
Olive oil	4 teaspoons	2 teaspoons	1 teaspoon

 Heat the water to boiling, remove from heat, add oil, and stir in mix. Cover with a lid, and let the mixture sit for 30 minutes to allow vegetables to hydrate. Bring mixture back to a boil, then turn down the heat, and cook for 30 minutes or until vegetables are tender. Add water if the soup is thicker than desired.

 Place water, oil, and mix in slow cooker. Turn on high for the first 30 minutes. Add additional water if needed, then turn down to low, and simmer until ready to eat.

This soup is good as is, or for a creamy consistency, use a traditional or stick blender and blend to a smooth consistency before serving.

Brazilian Black Bean Soup

Ingredients	6-8 Servings	3-4 Servings	1-2 Servings
Onion	1/4 cup	2 TBS	1 TBS
Carrots	1/4 cup	2 TBS	1 TBS
Garlic	4 teaspoons	2 teaspoons	1 teaspoon
Chicken bouillon	4 teaspoons	2 teaspoons	1 teaspoon
Mixed peppers	2 teaspoons	1 teaspoon	1/2 teaspoon
Cumin	1 teaspoon	1/2 teaspoon	1/4 teaspoon
Orange juice powder	4 teaspoons	2 teaspoons	1 teaspoon
Black beans	2 cups	1 cup	1/2 cup
Pepper	1/2 teaspoon	1/4 teaspoon	1/8 teaspoon
Salt (optional)	1/2 teaspoon	1/4 teaspoon	1/8 teaspoon
Water	8 cups	4 cups	2 cups
Olive oil	4 teaspoons	2 teaspoons	1 teaspoon

 Heat the water to boiling, remove from heat, add oil, and stir in mix. Cover with a lid, and let the mixture sit for 30 minutes to allow vegetables to hydrate. Bring mixture back to a boil, then turn down the heat, and cook for 30 minutes or until vegetables are tender. Add water if the soup is thicker than desired.

 Place water, oil, and mix in slow cooker. Turn on high for the first 30 minutes. Add additional water if needed, then turn down to low, and simmer until ready to eat.

This soup is good as is, or for a creamy consistency, use a traditional or stick blender and blend to a smooth consistency before serving.

Garbanzo Bean Soup Mixes

126

Garbanzo Beans

The soup mixes in this section all use garbanzo beans as their primary ingredient. Garbanzo beans (also known as chickpeas, Bengal grams, and Egyptian peas) provide a concentrated source of protein. They have a delicious nutlike taste and a texture that is buttery, yet somewhat starchy and pasty.

Garbanzo beans originated in the Middle East, and date back about seven thousand years. Garbanzo beans were first cultivated in the Mediterranean basin around 3000 BC. Their cultivation subsequently spread to India and Ethiopia. During the sixteenth century, garbanzo beans were brought to other subtropical regions of the world by both Spanish and Portuguese explorers. Today, the main commercial producers of garbanzos are India, Pakistan, Turkey, Ethiopia, and Mexico.

Garbanzo beans provide many health benefits, having positive effects on:

- digestive health.
- lowering the risk of colon cancer.
- providing unique supply of antioxidants.
- providing protection against cancers and heart disease.
- supporting cardiovascular health.
- lowering cholesterol and triglycerides.
- substantially lowering the risk of type 2 diabetes.
- preventing blood sugar levels from rising too high in people with diabetes.
- increasing satiety, resulting in decreased caloric intake.

Golden Garbanzo Soup

Ingredients	6-8 Servings	3-4 Servings	1-2 Servings
Garbanzo beans	2 cups	1 cup	1/2 cup
Onion	1/4 cup	2 TBS	1 TBS
Carrots	1/4 cup	2 TBS	1 TBS
Parsley	8 teaspoons	4 teaspoons	2 teaspoons
Garlic	4 teaspoons	2 teaspoons	1 teaspoon
Basil	1/2 teaspoon	1/4 teaspoon	1/8 teaspoon
Chicken bouillon	4 teaspoons	2 teaspoons	1 teaspoon
Pepper	1/2 teaspoon	1/4 teaspoon	1/8 teaspoon
Salt (optional)	1/2 teaspoon	1/4 teaspoon	1/8 teaspoon
Water	8 cups	4 cups	2 cups
Cooked ziti or tube pasta	2 cups	1 cup	1/2 cup

Heat the water to boiling, remove from heat and stir in mix. Cover with a lid, and let the mixture sit for 30 minutes to allow vegetables to hydrate. Bring mixture back to a boil, then turn down the heat, and cook for 30 minutes or until vegetables are tender. Add water if the soup is thicker than desired.

Place water and mix in slow cooker. Turn on high for the first 30 minutes. Add additional water if needed, then turn down to low, and simmer until ready to eat.

For a creamier soup, blend with a traditional or stick blender. Stir the drained pasta into the soup mixture and serve.

Lemony Garbanzo Soup

Ingredients	6-8 Servings	3-4 Servings	1-2 Servings
Garbanzo beans	2 cups	1 cup	1/2 cup
Ground turmeric	1 teaspoon	1/2 teaspoon	1/4 teaspoon
Cumin	1/2 teaspoon	1/4 teaspoon	1/8 teaspoon
Garlic	4 teaspoons	2 teaspoons	1 teaspoon
Mint	4 teaspoons	2 teaspoons	1 teaspoon
Cayenne pepper	1/2 teaspoon	1/4 teaspoon	1/8 teaspoon
Lemon juice powder	4 teaspoons	2 teaspoons	1 teaspoon
Lemon peel	2 teaspoons	1 teaspoon	1/2 teaspoon
Powdered eggs	4 teaspoons	2 teaspoons	1 teaspoon
Pepper	1/2 teaspoon	1/4 teaspoon	1/8 teaspoon
Salt (optional)	1/2 teaspoon	1/4 teaspoon	1/8 teaspoon
Water	8 cups	4 cups	2 cups

Heat the water to boiling, remove from heat and stir in mix. Cover with a lid, and let the mixture sit for 30 minutes to allow vegetables to hydrate. Bring mixture back to a boil, then turn down the heat, and cook for 30 minutes or until vegetables are tender. Add water if the soup is thicker than desired.

Place water and mix in slow cooker. Turn on high for the first 30 minutes. Add additional water if needed, then turn down to low, and simmer until ready to eat.

Tuscan Bean Soup

Ingredients	6-8 Servings	3-4 Servings	1-2 Servings
Spinach	8 teaspoons	4 teaspoons	2 teaspoons
Cabbage	8 teaspoons	4 teaspoons	2 teaspoons
Onion	8 teaspoons	4 teaspoons	2 teaspoons
Garlic	4 teaspoons	2 teaspoons	1 teaspoon
Chicken bouillon	4 teaspoons	2 teaspoons	1 teaspoon
Tomato dices	8 teaspoons	4 teaspoons	2 teaspoons
Tomato powder	1/4 cup	2 TBS	1 TBS
Sugar	4 teaspoons	2 teaspoons	1 teaspoon
Carrots	1/4 cup	2 TBS	1 TBS
Rosemary	1/2 teaspoon	1/4 teaspoon	1/8 teaspoon
Garbanzo beans	1 cup	1/2 cup	1/4 cup
Orzo pasta	1/2 cup	1/4 cup	2 TBS
Parsley	1/4 cup	2 TBS	1 TBS
Pepper	1/2 teaspoon	1/4 teaspoon	1/8 teaspoon
Salt (optional)	1/2 teaspoon	1/4 teaspoon	1/8 teaspoon
Water	8 cups	4 cups	2 cups
Olive oil	4 teaspoons	2 teaspoons	1 teaspoon
Parmesan cheese	1/4 cup	2 TBS	1 TBS

Heat the water to boiling, remove from heat, add oil, and stir in mix. Cover with a lid, and let the mixture sit for 30 minutes to allow vegetables to hydrate. Bring mixture back to a boil, then turn down the heat, and cook for 30 minutes or until vegetables are tender. Add water if the soup is thicker than desired. Top with parmesan cheese before serving.

Place water, oil, and mix in slow cooker. Turn on high for the first 30 minutes. Add additional water if needed, then turn down to low, and simmer until ready to eat. Top with parmesan cheese before serving.

Kidney Bean Soup Mixes

Kidney Beans

All of the soup mixes in this section use kidney beans as their primary ingredient. True to their name, these popular beans are kidney shaped and absorb the flavors of seasonings and the other foods with which they are cooked. Kidney beans provide many health benefits, having positive effects on:

- lowering cholesterol and triglycerides.
- substantially lowering the risk of type 2 diabetes.
- preventing blood sugar levels from rising too high in people with diabetes.
- providing the trace mineral, molybdenum, an integral component of the enzyme sulfite oxidase, which is responsible for detoxifying sulfites.
- promoting digestive health, actually preventing digestive disorders like irritable bowel syndrome and diverticulitis.
- providing protection against cancers and heart disease.
- supporting cardiovascular health.
- providing manganese for energy production and antioxidant defense.
- providing folate which helps lower the risk for heart attack, stroke, and peripheral vascular disease.
- increasing energy levels with slow burning carbohydrates and iron.
- maintaining memory with thiamin (vitamin B1).
- providing a unique supply of antioxidants.

Kidney Beans Soup

Ingredients	6-8 Servings	3-4 Servings	1-2 Servings
Onion	1/4 cup	2 TBS	1 TBS
Carrots	4 teaspoons	2 teaspoons	1 teaspoon
Celery	4 teaspoons	2 teaspoons	1 teaspoon
Potato dices	1/2 cup	1/4 cup	2 TBS
Beef bouillon	4 teaspoons	2 teaspoons	1 teaspoon
Kidney beans	1 cup	1/2 cup	1/4 cup
TVP ham bits	3/4 cup	6 TBS	3 TBS
Tomato powder	1/2 cup	1/4 cup	2 TBS
Sugar	2 teaspoons	1 teaspoon	1/2 teaspoon
Pepper	1/2 teaspoon	1/4 teaspoon	1/8 teaspoon
Salt (optional)	1/2 teaspoon	1/4 teaspoon	1/8 teaspoon
Water	8 cups	4 cups	2 cups
Canola oil	4 teaspoons	2 teaspoons	1 teaspoon

Heat the water to boiling, remove from heat, add oil, and stir in mix. Cover with a lid, and let the mixture sit for 30 minutes to allow vegetables to hydrate. Bring mixture back to a boil, then turn down the heat, and cook for 30 minutes or until vegetables are tender. Add water if the soup is thicker than desired.

Place water, oil, and mix in slow cooker. Turn on high for the first 30 minutes. Add additional water if needed, then turn down to low, and simmer until ready to eat.

Tuscan Kidney Beans Soup

Ingredients	6-8 Servings	3-4 Servings	1-2 Servings
Onion	4 teaspoons	2 teaspoons	1 teaspoon
Garlic	4 teaspoons	2 teaspoons	1 teaspoon
Mixed peppers	2 teaspoons	1 teaspoon	1/2 teaspoon
Spinach	4 teaspoons	2 teaspoons	1 teaspoon
Chicken bouillon	4 teaspoons	2 teaspoons	1 teaspoon
Small seashell pasta	1 cup	1/2 cup	1/4 cup
Kidney beans	3/4 cup	6 TBS	3 TBS
Thyme	2 teaspoons	1 teaspoon	1/2 teaspoon
Tomato powder	3/4 cup	6 TBS	3 TBS
Sugar	2 teaspoons	1 teaspoon	1/2 teaspoon
Pepper	1/2 teaspoon	1/4 teaspoon	1/8 teaspoon
Salt (optional)	1/2 teaspoon	1/4 teaspoon	1/8 teaspoon
Water	8 cups	4 cups	2 cups
Olive oil	4 teaspoons	2 teaspoons	1 teaspoon

134

Heat the water to boiling, remove from heat, add oil, and stir in mix. Cover with a lid, and let the mixture sit for 30 minutes to allow vegetables to hydrate. Bring mixture back to a boil, then turn down the heat, and cook for 30 minutes or until vegetables are tender. Add water if the soup is thicker than desired.

Place water, oil, and mix in slow cooker. Turn on high for the first 30 minutes. Add additional water if needed, then turn down to low, and simmer until ready to eat.

TVP Ham Kidney Beans Soup

Ingredients	6-8 Servings	3-4 Servings	1-2 Servings
TVP ham bits	1/4 cup	2 TBS	1 TBS
Potato dices	1/4 cup	2 TBS	1 TBS
Celery	2 teaspoons	1 teaspoon	1/2 teaspoon
Parsley	4 teaspoons	2 teaspoons	1 teaspoon
Kidney beans	3/4 cup	6 TBS	3 TBS
Tomato dices	1/2 cup	1/4 cup	2 TBS
Tomato powder	1 cup	1/2 cup	1/4 cup
Sugar	4 teaspoons	2 teaspoons	1 teaspoon
Cayenne pepper	1/2 teaspoon	1/4 teaspoon	1/8 teaspoon
Worcestershire powder	2 teaspoons	1 teaspoon	1/2 teaspoon
Pepper	1/2 teaspoon	1/4 teaspoon	1/8 teaspoon
Salt (optional)	1/2 teaspoon	1/4 teaspoon	1/8 teaspoon
Water	8 cups	4 cups	2 cups
Olive oil	4 teaspoons	2 teaspoons	1 teaspoon

Heat the water to boiling, remove from heat, add oil, and stir in mix. Cover with a lid, and let the mixture sit for 30 minutes to allow vegetables to hydrate. Bring mixture back to a boil, then turn down the heat, and cook for 30 minutes or until vegetables are tender. Add water if the soup is thicker than desired.

Place water, oil, and mix in slow cooker. Turn on high for the first 30 minutes. Add additional water if needed, then turn down to low, and simmer until ready to eat.

Spicy Kidney Beans Soup

Ingredients	6-8 Servings	3-4 Servings	1-2 Servings
Onion	4 teaspoons	2 teaspoons	1 teaspoon
Carrots	4 teaspoons	2 teaspoons	1 teaspoon
Celery	4 teaspoons	2 teaspoons	1 teaspoon
Garlic	4 teaspoons	2 teaspoons	1 teaspoon
Beef bouillon	4 teaspoons	2 teaspoons	1 teaspoon
Cumin	4 teaspoons	2 teaspoons	1 teaspoon
Kidney beans	1 cup	1/2 cup	1/4 cup
Chili powder	4 teaspoons	2 teaspoons	1 teaspoon
Oregano	1 teaspoon	1/2 teaspoon	1/4 teaspoon
Lime juice powder	1 TBS	1 1/2 teaspoon	3/4 teaspoon
Cilantro	1 TBS	1 1/2 teaspoon	3/4 teaspoon
Sour cream powder	1/4 cup	2 TBS	1 TBS
Tomato powder	1/4 cup	2 TBS	1 TBS
Sugar	1 teaspoon	1/2 teaspoon	1/4 teaspoon
Pepper	1/2 teaspoon	1/4 teaspoon	1/8 teaspoon
Salt (optional)	1/2 teaspoon	1/4 teaspoon	1/8 teaspoon
Water	8 cups	4 cups	2 cups
Canola oil	4 teaspoons	2 teaspoons	1 teaspoon

Heat the water to boiling, remove from heat, add oil, and stir in mix. Cover with a lid, and let the mixture sit for 30 minutes to allow vegetables to hydrate. Bring mixture back to a boil, then turn down the heat, and cook for 30 minutes or until vegetables are tender. Add water if the soup is thicker than desired.

Place water, oil, and mix in slow cooker. Turn on high for the first 30 minutes. Add additional water if needed, then turn down to low, and simmer until ready to eat.

Kidney Beans and Pasta Soup

Ingredients	6-8 Servings	3-4 Servings	1-2 Servings
Garlic	4 teaspoons	2 teaspoons	1 teaspoon
Mixed peppers	2 teaspoons	1 teaspoon	1/2 teaspoon
Macaroni pasta	3/4 cup	6 TBS	3 TBS
Kidney beans	3/4 cup	6 TBS	3 TBS
Italian seasoning	2 teaspoons	1 teaspoon	1/2 teaspoon
Parsley	4 teaspoons	2 teaspoons	1 teaspoon
Tomato dices	1/2 cup	1/4 cup	2 TBS
Tomato powder	3/4 cup	1/2 cup	1/4 cup
Sugar	4 teaspoons	2 teaspoons	1 teaspoon
Pepper	1/2 teaspoon	1/4 teaspoon	1/8 teaspoon
Salt (optional)	1/2 teaspoon	1/4 teaspoon	1/8 teaspoon
Water	8 cups	4 cups	2 cups
Olive oil	4 teaspoons	2 teaspoons	1 teaspoon

Heat the water to boiling, remove from heat, add oil, and stir in mix. Cover with a lid, and let the mixture sit for 30 minutes to allow vegetables to hydrate. Bring mixture back to a boil, then turn down the heat, and cook for 30 minutes or until vegetables are tender. Add water if the soup is thicker than desired.

Place water, oil, and mix in slow cooker. Turn on high for the first 30 minutes. Add additional water if needed, then turn down to low, and simmer until ready to eat.

Taco Soup

Ingredients	6-8 Servings	3-4 Servings	1-2 Servings
Garlic	2 teaspoons	1 teaspoon	1/2 teaspoon
Mixed peppers	2 teaspoons	1 teaspoon	1/2 teaspoon
Tubetti pasta	1/2 cup	1/4 cup	2 TBS
Kidney beans	1/4 cup	2 TBS	1 TBS
Black beans	1/4 cup	2 TBS	1 TBS
Corn	1/4 cup	2 TBS	1 TBS
Taco seasoning	4 teaspoons	2 teaspoons	1 teaspoon
TVP beef bits	1/2 cup	1/4 cup	2 TBS
Tomato dices	1/2 cup	1/4 cup	2 TBS
Tomato powder	1/2 cup	1/4 cup	2 TBS
Sugar	2 teaspoons	1 teaspoon	1/2 teaspoon
Pepper	1/2 teaspoon	1/4 teaspoon	1/8 teaspoon
Salt (optional)	1/2 teaspoon	1/4 teaspoon	1/8 teaspoon
Water	8 cups	4 cups	2 cups
Olive oil	4 teaspoons	2 teaspoons	1 teaspoon

 Heat the water to boiling, remove from heat, add oil, and stir in mix. Cover with a lid, and let the mixture sit for 30 minutes to allow vegetables to hydrate. Bring mixture back to a boil, then turn down the heat, and cook for 30 minutes or until vegetables are tender. Add water if the soup is thicker than desired.

Place water, oil, and mix in slow cooker. Turn on high for the first 30 minutes. Add additional water if needed, then turn down to low, and simmer until ready to eat.

Texan Bean Soup

Ingredients	6-8 Servings	3-4 Servings	1-2 Servings
Onion	4 TBS	2 TBS	1 TBS
Cumin	1 teaspoon	1/2 teaspoon	1/4 teaspoon
Cayenne pepper	1/2 teaspoon	1/4 teaspoon	1/8 teaspoon
TVP taco bits	1 cup	1/2 cup	1/4 cup
Tomato powder	4 TBS	2 TBS	1 TBS
Sugar	4 teaspoons	2 teaspoons	1 teaspoon
Ranch dressing mix	4 teaspoons	2 teaspoons	1 teaspoon
Corn	1/2 cup	1/4 cup	2 TBS
Kidney beans	1/2 cup	1/4 cup	2 TBS
Pinto beans	1/2 cup	1/4 cup	2 TBS
Black beans	1/2 cup	1/4 cup	2 TBS
Pepper	1/2 teaspoon	1/4 teaspoon	1/8 teaspoon
Salt (optional)	1/2 teaspoon	1/4 teaspoon	1/8 teaspoon
Water	8 cups	4 cups	2 cups
Canola oil	4 teaspoons	2 teaspoons	1 teaspoon

Heat the water to boiling, remove from heat, add oil, and stir in mix. Cover with a lid, and let the mixture sit for 30 minutes to allow vegetables to hydrate. Bring mixture back to a boil, then turn down the heat, and cook for 30 minutes or until vegetables are tender. Add water if the soup is thicker than desired. Serve with crispy tortillas, if desired.

Place water, oil, and mix in slow cooker. Turn on high for the first 30 minutes. Add additional water if needed, then turn down to low, and simmer until ready to eat. Serve with crispy tortillas, if desired.

Red Bean Soup

Ingredients	6-8 Servings	3-4 Servings	1-2 Servings
Red beans	1 cup	1/2 cup	1/4 cup
Split peas	1/2 cup	1/4 cup	2 TBS
TVP ham bits	1/2 cup	1/4 cup	2 TBS
Onion	1/4 cup	2 TBS	1 TBS
Potato dices	1 cup	1/2 cup	1/4 cup
Carrots	4 teaspoons	2 teaspoons	1 teaspoon
Tomato dices	1/4 cup	2 TBS	1 TBS
Leeks	4 teaspoons	2 teaspoons	1 teaspoon
Garlic	4 teaspoons	2 teaspoons	1 teaspoon
Pepper	1/2 teaspoon	1/4 teaspoon	1/8 teaspoon
Salt (optional)	1/2 teaspoon	1/4 teaspoon	1/8 teaspoon
Water	8 cups	4 cups	2 cups
Parmesan cheese	4 teaspoons	2 teaspoons	1 teaspoon

Heat the water to boiling, remove from heat, add oil, and stir in mix. Cover with a lid, and let the mixture sit for 30 minutes to allow vegetables to hydrate. Bring mixture back to a boil, then turn down the heat, and cook for 30 minutes or until vegetables are tender. Add water if the soup is thicker than desired. Top with parmesan cheese before serving.

Place water and mix in slow cooker. Turn on high for the first 30 minutes. Add additional water if needed, then turn down to low, and simmer until ready to eat. Top with parmesan cheese before serving.

Black and Red Bean Soup

Ingredients	6-8 Servings	3-4 Servings	1-2 Servings
Onion	1/4 cup	2 TBS	1 TBS
Celery	1 teaspoon	1/2 teaspoon	1/4 teaspoon
Carrots	1 teaspoon	1/2 teaspoon	1/4 teaspoon
Garlic powder	1 teaspoon	1/2 teaspoon	1/4 teaspoon
TVP taco bits	1/2 cup	1/4 cup	2 TBS
Cumin	2 teaspoons	1 teaspoon	1 teaspoon
Maple syrup powder	2 teaspoons	1 teaspoon	1 teaspoon
Sugar	2 teaspoons	1 teaspoon	1 teaspoon
Beef bouillon	4 teaspoons	2 teaspoons	1 teaspoon
Tomato dices	2 teaspoons	1 teaspoon	1 teaspoon
Tomato powder	2 teaspoons	1 teaspoon	1 teaspoon
Black beans	1/2 cup	1/4 cup	2 TBS
Red beans	1/2 cup	1/4 cup	2 TBS
Corn	1/2 cup	1/4 cup	2 TBS
Pepper	1/2 teaspoon	1/4 teaspoon	1/8 teaspoon
Water	8 cups	4 cups	2 cups
Canola oil	4 teaspoons	2 teaspoons	1 teaspoon

Heat the water to boiling, remove from heat, add oil, and stir in mix. Cover with a lid, and let the mixture sit for 30 minutes to allow vegetables to hydrate. Bring mixture back to a boil, then turn down the heat, and cook for 30 minutes or until vegetables are tender. Add water if the soup is thicker than desired.

Place water, oil, and mix in slow cooker. Turn on high for the first 30 minutes. Add additional water if needed, then turn down to low, and simmer until ready to eat.

Cajun Red Bean and Rice Soup

Ingredients	6-8 Servings	3-4 Servings	1-2 Servings
Onion	1/4 cup	2 TBS	1 TBS
Chives	1/4 cup	2 TBS	1 TBS
Mixed peppers	2 teaspoons	1 teaspoon	1/2 teaspoon
Garlic powder	1 teaspoon	1/2 teaspoon	1/4 teaspoon
TVP ham bits	1/2 cup	1/4 cup	2 TBS
Cajun seasoning	1 teaspoon	1/2 teaspoon	1/4 teaspoon
Worcestershire powder	1 teaspoon	1/2 teaspoon	1/4 teaspoon
Chicken bouillon	4 teaspoons	2 teaspoons	1 teaspoon
Red beans	3/4 cup	6 TBS	3 TBS
Rice	3/4 cup	6 TBS	3 TBS
Pepper	1/2 teaspoon	1/4 teaspoon	1/8 teaspoon
Salt (optional)	1/2 teaspoon	1/4 teaspoon	1/8 teaspoon
Water	8 cups	4 cups	2 cups
Canola oil	4 teaspoons	2 teaspoons	1 teaspoon

 Heat the water to boiling, remove from heat, add oil, and stir in mix. Cover with a lid, and let the mixture sit for 30 minutes to allow vegetables to hydrate. Bring mixture back to a boil, then turn down the heat, and cook for 30 minutes or until vegetables are tender. Add water if the soup is thicker than desired.

Place water, oil, and mix in slow cooker. Turn on high for the first 30 minutes. Add additional water if needed, then turn down to low, and simmer until ready to eat.

Cabbage and Bean Soup

Ingredients	6-8 Servings	3-4 Servings	1-2 Servings
Onion	1/4 cup	2 TBS	1 TBS
Cabbage	1 cup	1/2 cup	1/4 cup
Mixed peppers	2 teaspoons	1 teaspoon	1/2 teaspoon
Garlic powder	1 teaspoon	1/2 teaspoon	1/4 teaspoon
Cumin	2 teaspoons	1 teaspoon	1/2 teaspoon
TVP beef bits	1/2 cup	1/4 cup	2 TBS
Tomato dices	1/2 cup	1/4 cup	2 TBS
Tomato powder	1/2 cup	1/4 cup	2 TBS
Sugar	2 teaspoons	1 teaspoon	1/2 teaspoon
Beef bouillon	4 teaspoons	2 teaspoons	1 teaspoon
Red beans	1/2 cup	1/4 cup	2 TBS
Pepper	1/2 teaspoon	1/4 teaspoon	1/8 teaspoon
Salt (optional)	1/2 teaspoon	1/4 teaspoon	1/8 teaspoon
Water	8 cups	4 cups	2 cups
Canola oil	4 teaspoons	2 teaspoons	1 teaspoon

Heat the water to boiling, remove from heat, add oil, and stir in mix. Cover with a lid, and let the mixture sit for 30 minutes to allow vegetables to hydrate. Bring mixture back to a boil, then turn down the heat, and cook for 30 minutes or until vegetables are tender. Add water if the soup is thicker than desired.

Place water, oil, and mix in slow cooker. Turn on high for the first 30 minutes. Add additional water if needed, then turn down to low, and simmer until ready to eat.

Five Bean Soup

Ingredients	6-8 Servings	3-4 Servings	1-2 Servings
Cayenne pepper	1 teaspoon	1/2 teaspoon	1/4 teaspoon
Garlic	1 teaspoon	1/2 teaspoon	1/4 teaspoon
Chili powder	2 teaspoons	1 teaspoon	1/2 teaspoon
Oregano	1 teaspoon	1/2 teaspoon	1/4 teaspoon
Cumin	1/2 teaspoon	1/4 teaspoon	1/8 teaspoon
Pearl barley	4 teaspoons	2 teaspoons	1 teaspoon
Red beans	1/2 cup	1/4 cup	2 TBS
Navy beans	1/2 cup	1/4 cup	2 TBS
Garbanzo beans	1/2 cup	1/4 cup	2 TBS
Black Beans	1/2 cup	1/4 cup	2 TBS
Green beans	4 teaspoons	2 teaspoons	1 teaspoon
Beef bouillon	4 teaspoons	2 teaspoons	1 teaspoon
Pepper	1/2 teaspoon	1/4 teaspoon	1/8 teaspoon
Salt (optional)	1/2 teaspoon	1/4 teaspoon	1/8 teaspoon
Water	8 cups	4 cups	2 cups
Canola oil	4 teaspoons	2 teaspoons	1 teaspoon

Heat the water to boiling, remove from heat, add oil, and stir in mix. Cover with a lid, and let the mixture sit for 30 minutes to allow vegetables to hydrate. Bring mixture back to a boil, then turn down the heat, and cook for 30 minutes or until vegetables are tender. Add water if the soup is thicker than desired.

Place water, oil, and mix in slow cooker. Turn on high for the first 30 minutes. Add additional water if needed, then turn down to low, and simmer until ready to eat.

Lentil Soup Mixes

Lentils

The soup mixes in this section include lentils. Lentils are legumes that grow in pods, containing either one or two lentil seeds. Lentils are round, oval or heart-shaped disks and are oftentimes smaller than the tip of a pencil eraser.

Lentils are believed to have originated in central Asia, having been consumed since prehistoric times. They are one of the first foods to have ever been cultivated. Lentil seeds dating back 8,000 years have been found at archeological sites in the Middle East.

Lentils were mentioned in the Bible both as the item that Jacob traded to Esau for his birthright and as a part of the bread that was made during the Babylonian captivity of the Jewish people. Currently, the leading commercial producers of lentils include India, Turkey, Canada, China, and Syria.

Lentils provide many health benefits, having positive effects on:

- lowering cholesterol and triglycerides.
- substantially lowering the risk of type 2 diabetes.
- preventing blood sugar levels from rising too high in people with diabetes.
- providing protection against cancers and heart disease.
- supporting cardiovascular health.
- providing manganese for energy production and antioxidant defense.
- providing folate which helps lower the risk for heart attack, stroke, and peripheral vascular disease.
- increasing energy levels with slow burning carbohydrates and iron.
- providing the trace mineral, molybdenum, an integral component of the enzyme sulfite oxidase, which is responsible for detoxifying sulfites.

Classic Lentil Soup

Ingredients	6-8 Servings	3-4 Servings	1-2 Servings
Onion	4 teaspoons	2 teaspoons	1 teaspoon
Carrots	4 teaspoons	2 teaspoons	1 teaspoon
Celery	4 teaspoons	2 teaspoons	1 teaspoon
Spinach	4 teaspoons	2 teaspoons	1 teaspoon
Tomato dices	1/3 cup	8 teaspoons	4 teaspoons
Tomato powder	1/4 cup	2 TBS	1 TBS
Sugar	2 teaspoons	1 teaspoon	1/2 teaspoon
Garlic	4 teaspoons	2 teaspoons	1 teaspoon
Oregano	2 teaspoons	1 teaspoon	1/2 teaspoon
Basil	2 teaspoons	1 teaspoon	1/2 teaspoon
Lentils	1 cup	1/2 cup	1/4 cup
Vinegar powder	4 teaspoons	2 teaspoons	1 teaspoon
Pepper	1/2 teaspoon	1/4 teaspoon	1/8 teaspoon
Salt (optional)	1/2 teaspoon	1/4 teaspoon	1/8 teaspoon
Water	8 cups	4 cups	2 cups
Olive oil	4 teaspoons	2 teaspoons	1 teaspoon

Heat the water to boiling, remove from heat, add oil, and stir in mix. Cover with a lid, and let the mixture sit for 30 minutes to allow vegetables to hydrate. Bring mixture back to a boil, then turn down the heat, and cook for 30 minutes or until vegetables are tender. Add water if the soup is thicker than desired.

Place water, oil, and mix in slow cooker. Turn on high for the first 30 minutes. Add additional water if needed, then turn down to low, and simmer until ready to eat.

Lemony Lentil Soup

Ingredients	6-8 Servings	3-4 Servings	1-2 Servings
Onion	1/4 cup	2 TBS	1 TBS
Parsley	4 teaspoons	2 teaspoons	1 teaspoon
Thyme	4 teaspoons	2 teaspoons	1 teaspoon
Spinach	4 teaspoons	2 teaspoons	1 teaspoon
Cabbage	4 teaspoons	2 teaspoons	1 teaspoon
Broccoli	4 teaspoons	2 teaspoons	1 teaspoon
Garlic	4 teaspoons	2 teaspoons	1 teaspoon
Cilantro	1 teaspoon	1/2 teaspoon	1/4 teaspoon
Lemon juice powder	4 teaspoons	2 teaspoons	1 teaspoon
Lemon peel	1 teaspoon	1/2 teaspoon	1/4 teaspoon
Lentils	1 cup	1/2 cup	1/4 cup
Pepper	1/2 teaspoon	1/4 teaspoon	1/8 teaspoon
Salt (optional)	1/2 teaspoon	1/4 teaspoon	1/8 teaspoon
Water	8 cups	4 cups	2 cups
Olive oil	4 teaspoons	2 teaspoons	1 teaspoon

Heat the water to boiling, remove from heat, add oil, and stir in mix. Cover with a lid, and let the mixture sit for 30 minutes to allow vegetables to hydrate. Bring mixture back to a boil, then turn down the heat, and cook for 30 minutes or until vegetables are tender. Add water if the soup is thicker than desired.

Place water, oil, and mix in slow cooker. Turn on high for the first 30 minutes. Add additional water if needed, then turn down to low, and simmer until ready to eat.

Garlic Tomato Lentil Soup

Ingredients	6-8 Servings	3-4 Servings	1-2 Servings
Onion	1/4 cup	2 TBS	1 TBS
Carrots	4 teaspoons	2 teaspoons	1 teaspoon
Celery	4 teaspoons	2 teaspoons	1 teaspoon
Spinach	1/4 cup	2 TBS	1 TBS
Tomato dices	1/3 cup	8 teaspoons	4 teaspoons
Tomato powder	1/4 cup	2 TBS	1 TBS
Sugar	2 teaspoons	1 teaspoon	1/2 teaspoon
Garlic	4 teaspoons	2 teaspoons	1 teaspoon
Basil	4 teaspoons	2 teaspoons	1 teaspoon
Vinegar powder	4 teaspoons	2 teaspoons	1 teaspoon
Lentils	1 cup	1/2 cup	1/4 cup
Pepper	1/2 teaspoon	1/4 teaspoon	1/8 teaspoon
Salt (optional)	1/2 teaspoon	1/4 teaspoon	1/8 teaspoon
Water	8 cups	4 cups	2 cups
Olive oil	4 teaspoons	2 teaspoons	1 teaspoon

Heat the water to boiling, remove from heat, add oil, and stir in mix. Cover with a lid, and let the mixture sit for 30 minutes to allow vegetables to hydrate. Bring mixture back to a boil, then turn down the heat, and cook for 30 minutes or until vegetables are tender. Add water if the soup is thicker than desired.

Place water, oil, and mix in slow cooker. Turn on high for the first 30 minutes. Add additional water if needed, then turn down to low, and simmer until ready to eat.

Herb Tomato Lentil Soup

Ingredients	6-8 Servings	3-4 Servings	1-2 Servings
Onion	1/4 cup	2 TBS	1 TBS
Carrots	4 teaspoons	2 teaspoons	1 teaspoon
Celery	4 teaspoons	2 teaspoons	1 teaspoon
Spinach	1/4 cup	2 TBS	1 TBS
Tomato dices	1/3 cup	8 teaspoons	4 teaspoons
Tomato powder	1/4 cup	2 TBS	1 TBS
Sugar	2 teaspoons	1 teaspoon	1/2 teaspoon
Garlic	4 teaspoons	2 teaspoons	1 teaspoon
Basil	4 teaspoons	2 teaspoons	1 teaspoon
Oregano	4 teaspoons	2 teaspoons	1 teaspoon
Parsley	4 teaspoons	2 teaspoons	1 teaspoon
Lentils	1 cup	1/2 cup	1/4 cup
Pepper	1/2 teaspoon	1/4 teaspoon	1/8 teaspoon
Salt (optional)	1/2 teaspoon	1/4 teaspoon	1/8 teaspoon
Water	8 cups	4 cups	2 cups
Olive oil	4 teaspoons	2 teaspoons	1 teaspoon

Heat the water to boiling, remove from heat, add oil, and stir in mix. Cover with a lid, and let the mixture sit for 30 minutes to allow vegetables to hydrate. Bring mixture back to a boil, then turn down the heat, and cook for 30 minutes or until vegetables are tender. Add water if the soup is thicker than desired.

Place water, oil, and mix in slow cooker. Turn on high for the first 30 minutes. Add additional water if needed, then turn down to low, and simmer until ready to eat.

Moroccan Lentil Soup

Ingredients	6-8 Servings	3-4 Servings	1-2 Servings
Onion	1/4 cup	2 TBS	1 TBS
Carrots	4 teaspoons	2 teaspoons	1 teaspoon
Celery	4 teaspoons	2 teaspoons	1 teaspoon
Tomato dices	1/3 cup	8 teaspoons	4 teaspoons
Tomato powder	1/4 cup	2 TBS	1 TBS
Sugar	4 teaspoons	2 teaspoons	1 teaspoon
Garlic	4 teaspoons	2 teaspoons	1 teaspoon
Ginger	2 teaspoons	1 teaspoon	1/2 teaspoon
Cloves	2 teaspoons	1 teaspoon	1/2 teaspoon
Cinnamon	2 teaspoons	1 teaspoon	1/2 teaspoon
Cumin	2 teaspoons	1 teaspoon	1/2 teaspoon
Ground Cardamom	2 teaspoons	1 teaspoon	1/2 teaspoon
Lentils	1/2 cup	1/4 cup	2 TBS
Garbanzo beans	1/2 cup	1/4 cup	2 TBS
Pepper	1 teaspoon	1/2 teaspoon	1/4 teaspoon
Salt (optional)	1/2 teaspoon	1/4 teaspoon	1/8 teaspoon
Water	8 cups	4 cups	2 cups
Olive oil	4 teaspoons	2 teaspoons	1 teaspoon

Heat the water to boiling, remove from heat, add oil, and stir in mix. Cover with a lid, and let the mixture sit for 30 minutes to allow vegetables to hydrate. Bring mixture back to a boil, then turn down the heat, and cook for 30 minutes or until vegetables are tender. Add water if the soup is thicker than desired.

Place water, oil, and mix in slow cooker. Turn on high for the first 30 minutes. Add additional water if needed, then turn down to low, and simmer until ready to eat.

Smoky Sage Lentil Soup

Ingredients	6-8 Servings	3-4 Servings	1-2 Servings
Onion	4 teaspoons	2 teaspoons	1 teaspoon
Carrots	4 teaspoons	2 teaspoons	1 teaspoon
Celery	4 teaspoons	2 teaspoons	1 teaspoon
Tomato dices	1/2 cup	1/4 cup	2 TBS
Tomato powder	1/2 cup	1/4 cup	2 TBS
Sugar	4 teaspoons	2 teaspoons	1 teaspoon
Garlic	4 teaspoons	2 teaspoons	1 teaspoon
Sage	2 teaspoons	1 teaspoon	1/2 teaspoon
Vegetable bouillon	4 teaspoons	2 teaspoons	1 teaspoon
Hickory smoke powder	2 teaspoons	1 teaspoon	1/2 teaspoon
Italian seasoning	4 teaspoons	2 teaspoons	1 teaspoon
Lentils	1 cup	1/2 cup	1/4 cup
Pepper	1 teaspoon	1/2 teaspoon	1/4 teaspoon
Salt (optional)	1/2 teaspoon	1/4 teaspoon	1/8 teaspoon
Water	8 cups	4 cups	2 cups
Olive oil	4 teaspoons	2 teaspoons	1 teaspoon

Heat the water to boiling, remove from heat, add oil, and stir in mix. Cover with a lid, and let the mixture sit for 30 minutes to allow vegetables to hydrate. Bring mixture back to a boil, then turn down the heat, and cook for 30 minutes or until vegetables are tender. Add water if the soup is thicker than desired.

Place water, oil, and mix in slow cooker. Turn on high for the first 30 minutes. Add additional water if needed, then turn down to low, and simmer until ready to eat.

Spicy Lentil Soup

Ingredients	6-8 Servings	3-4 Servings	1-2 Servings
Onion	1/3 cup	8 teaspoons	4 teaspoons
Cilantro	1 TBS	1 1/2 teaspoon	3/4 teaspoon
Turmeric	1 teaspoon	1/2 teaspoon	1/4 teaspoon
Tomato dices	1/3 cup	3 TBS	4 teaspoons
Tomato powder	1/4 cup	2 TBS	1 TBS
Sugar	1 TBS	1 1/2 teaspoon	3/4 teaspoon
Garlic	4 teaspoons	2 teaspoons	1 teaspoon
Ginger	1 teaspoon	1/2 teaspoon	1/4 teaspoon
Vegetable bouillon	4 teaspoons	2 teaspoons	1 teaspoon
Chili powder	1 teaspoon	1/2 teaspoon	1/4 teaspoon
Cayenne pepper flakes	1/2 teaspoon	1/4 teaspoon	1/8 teaspoon
Lentils	2 cups	1 cup	1/2 cup
Pepper	1/2 teaspoon	1/4 teaspoon	1/8 teaspoon
Salt (optional)	1/2 teaspoon	1/4 teaspoon	1/8 teaspoon
Water	8 cups	4 cups	2 cups
Olive oil	4 teaspoons	2 teaspoons	1 teaspoon

 Heat the water to boiling, remove from heat, add oil, and stir in mix. Cover with a lid, and let the mixture sit for 30 minutes to allow vegetables to hydrate. Bring mixture back to a boil, then turn down the heat, and cook for 30 minutes or until vegetables are tender. Add water if the soup is thicker than desired.

Place water, oil, and mix in slow cooker. Turn on high for the first 30 minutes. Add additional water if needed, then turn down to low, and simmer until ready to eat.

TVP Chicken Lentil Soup

Ingredients	6-8 Servings	3-4 Servings	1-2 Servings
Onion	1/4 cup	2 TBS	1 TBS
Carrots	4 teaspoons	2 teaspoons	1 teaspoon
Cabbage	4 teaspoons	2 teaspoons	1 teaspoon
Spinach	4 teaspoons	2 teaspoons	1 teaspoon
Curry powder	4 teaspoons	2 teaspoons	1 teaspoon
Garlic	4 teaspoons	2 teaspoons	1 teaspoon
Thyme	1 teaspoon	1/2 teaspoon	1/4 teaspoon
Lemon peel	1 teaspoon	1/2 teaspoon	1/4 teaspoon
Lentils	2 cups	1 cup	1/2 cup
TVP chicken chunks	1 cup	1/2 cup	1/4 cup
Pepper	1/2 teaspoon	1/4 teaspoon	1/8 teaspoon
Salt (optional)	1/2 teaspoon	1/4 teaspoon	1/8 teaspoon
Water	8 cups	4 cups	2 cups
Olive oil	4 teaspoons	2 teaspoons	1 teaspoon

Heat the water to boiling, remove from heat, add oil, and stir in mix. Cover with a lid, and let the mixture sit for 30 minutes to allow vegetables to hydrate. Bring mixture back to a boil, then turn down the heat, and cook for 30 minutes or until vegetables are tender. Add water if the soup is thicker than desired.

Place water, oil, and mix in slow cooker. Turn on high for the first 30 minutes. Add additional water if needed, then turn down to low, and simmer until ready to eat.

154

Navy Bean
Soup Mixes

Navy Beans

The soup mixes in this section include navy beans as their primary ingredient. The navy bean got its current popular name because it was a staple food of the United States Navy in the early twentieth century. Navy beans are small, pea-sized beans that are creamy white in color. They are mild-flavored beans that are dense and smooth.

The navy bean originated in Peru. From there, the navy bean spread throughout South and Central America by migrating Indian trades. They were introduced into Europe in the fifteenth century by Spanish explorers returning from their voyages to the New World. Spanish and Portuguese explorers brought them to Africa and Asia. Today, the largest commercial producers of the navy bean are India, China, Indonesia, Brazil, and the United States.

Navy beans provide many health benefits, having positive effects on:

- lowering cholesterol and triglycerides.
- substantially lowering the risk of type 2 diabetes.
- preventing blood sugar levels from rising too high in people with diabetes.
- providing protection against cancers and heart disease.
- supporting cardiovascular health.
- supporting digestive tract health.
- providing copper and manganese for energy production and antioxidant defense.
- providing folate which helps lower the risk for heart attack, stroke, and peripheral vascular disease.
- increasing energy levels with slow-burning carbohydrates and iron.
- supporting flexibility in blood vessels, bones, and joints.
- maintaining memory with thiamin (vitamin B1).

Navy Bean Soup

Ingredients	6-8 Servings	3-4 Servings	1-2 Servings
Navy beans	1 cup	1/2 cup	1/4 cup
TVP ham bits	3/4 cup	6 TBS	3 TBS
Garlic	4 teaspoons	2 teaspoons	1 teaspoon
Onion	1/4 cup	2 TBS	1 TBS
Potato dices	1/4 cup	2 TBS	1 TBS
Celery	4 teaspoons	2 teaspoons	1 teaspoon
Carrots	4 teaspoons	2 teaspoons	1 teaspoon
Pepper	1/2 teaspoon	1/4 teaspoon	1/8 teaspoon
Salt (optional)	1/2 teaspoon	1/4 teaspoon	1/8 teaspoon
Water	8 cups	4 cups	2 cups
Olive oil	4 teaspoons	2 teaspoons	1 teaspoon

Heat the water to boiling, remove from heat, add oil, and stir in mix. Cover with a lid, and let the mixture sit for 30 minutes to allow vegetables to hydrate. Bring mixture back to a boil, then turn down the heat, and cook for 30 minutes or until vegetables are tender. Add water if the soup is thicker than desired.

Place water, oil, and mix in slow cooker. Turn on high for the first 30 minutes. Add additional water if needed, then turn down to low, and simmer until ready to eat.

Barbequed Northern Bean Soup

Ingredients	6-8 Servings	3-4 Servings	1-2 Servings
Northern beans	2 cup	1 cup	1/2 cup
TVP beef bits	1/2 cup	1/4 cup	2 TBS
Beef bouillon	4 teaspoons	2 teaspoons	1 teaspoon
Onion	1/4 cup	2 TBS	1 TBS
Vinegar powder	4 teaspoons	2 teaspoons	1 teaspoon
Mustard powder	1/2 teaspoon	1/4 teaspoon	1/8 teaspoon
Red wine powder	4 teaspoons	2 teaspoons	1 teaspoon
Garlic	4 teaspoons	2 teaspoons	1 teaspoon
Cayenne pepper	1 teaspoon	1/2 teaspoon	1/4 teaspoon
Tomato powder	3/4 cup	6 TBS	3 TBS
Brown sugar	4 teaspoons	2 teaspoons	1 teaspoon
Pepper	1/2 teaspoon	1/4 teaspoon	1/8 teaspoon
Salt (optional)	1/2 teaspoon	1/4 teaspoon	1/8 teaspoon
Water	8 cups	4 cups	2 cups
Olive oil	4 teaspoons	2 teaspoons	1 teaspoon

 Heat the water to boiling, remove from heat, add oil, barbeque sauce, and stir in mix. Cover with a lid, and let the mixture sit for 30 minutes to allow vegetables to hydrate. Bring mixture back to a boil, then turn down the heat, and cook for 30 minutes or until vegetables are tender. Add water if the soup is thicker than desired.

Place water, oil, barbeque sauce, and mix in slow cooker. Turn on high for the first 30 minutes. Add additional water if needed, then turn down to low, and simmer until ready to eat.

TVP Ham Bean Soup

Ingredients	6-8 Servings	3-4 Servings	1-2 Servings
Navy beans	2 cups	1 cup	1/2 cup
Beef bouillon	4 teaspoons	2 teaspoons	1 teaspoon
Onion	1/4 cup	2 TBS	1 TBS
Celery	1/4 cup	2 TBS	1 TBS
Carrots	1/4 cup	2 TBS	1 TBS
TVP ham bits	1/2 cup	1/4 cup	2 TBS
Parsley	1 teaspoon	1/2 teaspoon	1/4 teaspoon
All purpose flour	4 teaspoons	2 teaspoons	1 teaspoon
Tomato powder	1/4 cup	2 TBS	1 TBS
Sugar	4 teaspoons	2 teaspoons	1 teaspoon
Vinegar powder	4 teaspoons	2 teaspoons	1 teaspoon
Pepper	1/2 teaspoon	1/4 teaspoon	1/8 teaspoon
Salt (optional)	1/2 teaspoon	1/4 teaspoon	1/8 teaspoon
Water	8 cups	4 cups	2 cups
Canola oil	4 teaspoons	2 teaspoons	1 teaspoon

Heat the water to boiling, remove from heat and stir in mix. Let mixture sit for 30 minutes to allow vegetables to hydrate. Add canola oil and bring mixture back to a boil. Mix flour salt and pepper with several tablespoons of water. Add to mixture stir to thicken and cook for 30 minutes.

Place water and mix in slow cooker. Turn on high for the first 30 minutes. Add canola oil and bring mixture back to a boil. Mix flour salt and pepper with several tablespoons of water—mix thoroughly. Turn down to low, and simmer until ready to eat.

Hearty Navy Bean Soup

Ingredients	6-8 Servings	3-4 Servings	1-2 Servings
Navy beans	2 cups	1 cup	1/2 cup
TVP ham bits	1/2 cup	1/4 cup	2 TBS
Onion	1/4 cup	2 TBS	1 TBS
Parsley	1/4 cup	2 TBS	1 TBS
Basil	2 teaspoons	1 teaspoon	1/2 teaspoon
Nutmeg	1/2 teaspoon	1/4 teaspoon	1/8 teaspoon
Oregano	2 teaspoons	1 teaspoon	1/2 teaspoon
Carrots	1/4 cup	2 TBS	1 TBS
Celery	1/4 cup	2 TBS	1 TBS
Garlic	4 teaspoons	2 teaspoons	1 teaspoon
Instant potato flakes	1/4 cup	2 TBS	1 TBS
Pepper	1 teaspoon	1/2 teaspoon	1/4 teaspoon
Salt (optional)	1/2 teaspoon	1/4 teaspoon	1/8 teaspoon
Water	8 cups	4 cups	2 cups

Heat the water to boiling, remove from heat, and stir in mix. Cover with a lid, and let the mixture sit for 30 minutes to allow vegetables to hydrate. Bring mixture back to a boil, then turn down the heat, and cook for 30 minutes or until vegetables are tender. Add water if the soup is thicker than desired.

Place water and mix in slow cooker. Turn on high for the first 30 minutes. Add additional water if needed, then turn down to low, and simmer until ready to eat.

TVP Ham, Pasta, and Bean Soup

Ingredients	6-8 Servings	3-4 Servings	1-2 Servings
TVP ham bits	1/4 cup	2 TBS	1 TBS
Navy beans	1 cup	1/2 cup	1/4 cup
Onion	4 teaspoons	2 teaspoons	1 teaspoon
Celery	4 teaspoons	2 teaspoons	1 teaspoon
Carrots	4 teaspoons	2 teaspoons	1 teaspoon
Garlic	4 teaspoons	2 teaspoons	1 teaspoon
Cayenne pepper	1/2 teaspoon	1/4 teaspoon	1/8 teaspoon
Tomato dices	1/4 cup	2 TBS	1 TBS
Tomato powder	1/2 cup	1/4 cup	2 TBS
Sugar	2 teaspoons	1 teaspoon	1/2 teaspoon
Chicken bouillon	4 teaspoons	2 teaspoons	1 teaspoon
Pepper	1/2 teaspoon	1/4 teaspoon	1/8 teaspoon
Salt (optional)	1/2 teaspoon	1/4 teaspoon	1/8 teaspoon
Water	8 cups	4 cups	2 cups
Cooked small pasta	4 cups	2 cups	1 cup
Parmesan cheese	1/4 cup	2 TBS	1 TBS

Heat the water to boiling, remove from heat and stir in mix. Cover with a lid, and let the mixture sit for 30 minutes to allow vegetables to hydrate. Bring mixture back to a boil, then turn down the heat, and cook for 30 minutes or until vegetables are tender. Add water if the soup is thicker than desired. Stir drained pasta into cooked mixture. Top with parmesan cheese before serving.

Place water and mix in slow cooker. Turn on high for the first 30 minutes. Add additional water if needed, then turn down to low, and simmer until ready to eat. Stir drained pasta into cooked mixture. Top with parmesan cheese before serving.

TVP Chicken White Bean Soup

Ingredients	6-8 Servings	3-4 Servings	1-2 Servings
TVP chicken chunks	2 cups	1 cup	1/2 cup
Chicken bouillon	4 teaspoons	2 teaspoons	1 teaspoon
Garlic	4 teaspoons	2 teaspoons	1 teaspoon
Cumin	2 teaspoons	1 teaspoon	1/2 teaspoon
Corn	1/3 cup	8 teaspoons	4 teaspoons
Navy beans	1 cup	1/2 cup	1/4 cup
Onion	4 teaspoons	2 teaspoons	1 teaspoon
Cilantro	1/2 teaspoon	1/4 teaspoon	1/8 teaspoon
Tomato dices	8 teaspoons	4 teaspoons	2 teaspoons
Tomato powder	1/4 cup	2 TBS	1 TBS
Mixed peppers	2 teaspoons	1 teaspoon	1/2 teaspoon
Sugar	2 teaspoons	1 teaspoon	1/2 teaspoon
Vinegar powder	4 teaspoons	2 teaspoons	1 teaspoon
Pepper	1/2 teaspoon	1/4 teaspoon	1/8 teaspoon
Salt (optional)	1/2 teaspoon	1/4 teaspoon	1/8 teaspoon
Water	8 cups	4 cups	2 cups
Canola oil	4 teaspoons	2 teaspoons	1 teaspoon

Heat the water to boiling, remove from heat, add oil, salsa, and stir in mix. Cover with a lid, and let the mixture sit for 30 minutes to allow vegetables to hydrate. Bring mixture back to a boil, then turn down the heat, and cook for 30 minutes or until vegetables are tender. Add water if the soup is thicker than desired.

Place water and mix in Slow cooker. Stir in oil and salsa. Turn on high for the first 30 minutes. Add additional water if needed, then turn down to low, and simmer until ready to eat.

TVP Ham White Bean Soup

Ingredients	6-8 Servings	3-4 Servings	1-2 Servings
TVP ham bits	3/4 cup	6 TBS	3 TBS
Onion	4 teaspoons	2 teaspoons	1 teaspoon
Carrots	4 teaspoons	2 teaspoons	1 teaspoon
Celery	4 teaspoons	2 teaspoons	1 teaspoon
Garlic	4 teaspoons	2 teaspoons	1 teaspoon
Rosemary	2 teaspoons	1 teaspoon	1/2 teaspoon
Thyme	2 teaspoons	1 teaspoon	1/2 teaspoon
Northern beans	1 cup	1/2 cup	1/4 cup
Chicken bouillon	4 teaspoons	2 teaspoons	1 teaspoon
Pepper	1/2 teaspoon	1/4 teaspoon	1/8 teaspoon
Salt (optional)	1/2 teaspoon	1/4 teaspoon	1/8 teaspoon
Water	8 cups	4 cups	2 cups
Olive oil	4 teaspoons	2 teaspoons	1 teaspoon

Heat the water to boiling, remove from heat, add oil, and stir in mix. Cover with a lid, and let the mixture sit for 30 minutes to allow vegetables to hydrate. Bring mixture back to a boil, then turn down the heat, and cook for 30 minutes or until vegetables are tender. Add water if the soup is thicker than desired.

Place water, oil, and mix in slow cooker. Turn on high for the first 30 minutes. Add additional water if needed, then turn down to low, and simmer until ready to eat.

Savory Navy Bean Soup

Ingredients	6-8 Servings	3-4 Servings	1-2 Servings
Onion	1/4 cup	2 TBS	1 TBS
Garlic	4 teaspoons	2 teaspoons	1 teaspoon
Celery	2 teaspoons	1 teaspoon	1/2 teaspoon
Worcestershire powder	2 teaspoons	1 teaspoon	1/2 teaspoon
Parsley	4 teaspoons	2 teaspoons	1 teaspoon
TVP ham bits	1/2 cup	1/4 cup	2 TBS
Tomato dices	1/4 cup	2 TBS	1 TBS
Tomato powder	1/4 cup	2 TBS	1 TBS
Sugar	2 teaspoons	1 teaspoon	1/2 teaspoon
Chicken bouillon	4 teaspoons	2 teaspoons	1 teaspoon
Navy beans	1 cup	1/2 cup	1/4 cup
Pepper	1/2 teaspoon	1/4 teaspoon	1/8 teaspoon
Salt (optional)	1/2 teaspoon	1/4 teaspoon	1/8 teaspoon
Water	8 cups	4 cups	2 cups
Canola oil	4 teaspoons	2 teaspoons	1 teaspoon

 Heat the water to boiling, remove from heat, add oil, and stir in mix. Cover with a lid, and let the mixture sit for 30 minutes to allow vegetables to hydrate. Bring mixture back to a boil, then turn down the heat, and cook for 30 minutes or until vegetables are tender. Add water if the soup is thicker than desired.

Place water, oil, and mix in slow cooker. Turn on high for the first 30 minutes. Add additional water if needed, then turn down to low, and simmer until ready to eat.

Buttery Navy Bean Soup

Ingredients	6-8 Servings	3-4 Servings	1-2 Servings
Onion	1/4 cup	2 TBS	1 TBS
Garlic	4 teaspoons	2 teaspoons	1 teaspoon
Carrots	4 teaspoons	2 teaspoons	1 teaspoon
TVP ham bits	3/4 cup	6 TBS	3 TBS
Chicken bouillon	4 teaspoons	2 teaspoons	1 teaspoon
Butter powder	1/2 cup	1/4 cup	2 TBS
Navy beans	2 cups	1 cup	1/2 cup
Pepper	1/2 teaspoon	1/4 teaspoon	1/8 teaspoon
Salt (optional)	1/2 teaspoon	1/4 teaspoon	1/8 teaspoon
Water	8 cups	4 cups	2 cups
Canola oil	4 teaspoons	2 teaspoons	1 teaspoon

Heat the water to boiling, remove from heat, add oil, and stir in mix. Cover with a lid, and let the mixture sit for 30 minutes to allow vegetables to hydrate. Bring mixture back to a boil, then turn down the heat, and cook for 30 minutes or until vegetables are tender. Add water if the soup is thicker than desired.

Place water, oil, and mix in slow cooker. Turn on high for the first 30 minutes. Add additional water if needed, then turn down to low, and simmer until ready to eat.

Basic Navy Bean Soup

Ingredients	6-8 Servings	3-4 Servings	1-2 Servings
Onion	1/4 cup	2 TBS	1 TBS
Celery	4 teaspoons	2 teaspoons	1 teaspoon
Carrots	4 teaspoons	2 teaspoons	1 teaspoon
TVP ham bits	3/4 cup	6 TBS	3 TBS
Chicken bouillon	4 teaspoons	2 teaspoons	1 teaspoon
Navy beans	2 cups	1 cup	1/2 cup
Pepper	1/2 teaspoon	1/4 teaspoon	1/8 teaspoon
Salt (optional)	1/2 teaspoon	1/4 teaspoon	1/8 teaspoon
Water	8 cups	4 cups	2 cups
Canola oil	4 teaspoons	2 teaspoons	1 teaspoon

Heat the water to boiling, remove from heat, add oil, and stir in mix. Cover with a lid, and let the mixture sit for 30 minutes to allow vegetables to hydrate. Bring mixture back to a boil, then turn down the heat, and cook for 30 minutes or until vegetables are tender. Add water if the soup is thicker than desired.

Place water, oil, and mix in slow cooker. Turn on high for the first 30 minutes. Add additional water if needed, then turn down to low, and simmer until ready to eat.

Scrumptious Navy Bean Soup

Ingredients	6-8 Servings	3-4 Servings	1-2 Servings
Onion	1/4 cup	2 TBS	1 TBS
Parsley	4 teaspoons	2 teaspoons	1 teaspoon
Celery	4 teaspoons	2 teaspoons	1 teaspoon
Carrots	2 teaspoons	1 teaspoon	1/2 teaspoon
Oregano	2 teaspoons	1 teaspoon	1/2 teaspoon
Basil	4 teaspoons	2 teaspoons	1 teaspoon
Nutmeg	1/2 teaspoon	1/4 teaspoon	1/8 teaspoon
Instant potato flakes	1/4 cup	2 TBS	1 TBS
TVP ham bits	3/4 cup	6 TBS	3 TBS
Chicken bouillon	4 teaspoons	2 teaspoons	1 teaspoon
Navy beans	1 cup	1/2 cup	1/4 cup
Pepper	1/2 teaspoon	1/4 teaspoon	1/8 teaspoon
Salt (optional)	1/2 teaspoon	1/4 teaspoon	1/8 teaspoon
Water	8 cups	4 cups	2 cups
Canola oil	4 teaspoons	2 teaspoons	1 teaspoon

 Heat the water to boiling, remove from heat, add oil, and stir in mix. Cover with a lid, and let the mixture sit for 30 minutes to allow vegetables to hydrate. Bring mixture back to a boil, then turn down the heat, and cook for 30 minutes or until vegetables are tender. Add water if the soup is thicker than desired.

Place water, oil, and mix in slow cooker. Turn on high for the first 30 minutes. Add additional water if needed, then turn down to low, and simmer until ready to eat.

Southern Navy Bean Soup

Ingredients	6-8 Servings	3-4 Servings	1-2 Servings
Onion	1/4 cup	2 TBS	1 TBS
Celery	4 teaspoons	2 teaspoons	1 teaspoon
Carrots	4 teaspoons	2 teaspoons	1 teaspoon
Potato dices	1/4 cup	2 TBS	1 TBS
TVP ham bits	3/4 cup	6 TBS	3 TBS
Navy beans	2 cups	1 cup	1/2 cup
Pepper	1/2 teaspoon	1/4 teaspoon	1/8 teaspoon
Salt (optional)	1/2 teaspoon	1/4 teaspoon	1/8 teaspoon
Water	8 cups	4 cups	2 cups
Canola oil	4 teaspoons	2 teaspoons	1 teaspoon

Heat the water to boiling, remove from heat, add oil, and stir in mix. Cover with a lid, and let the mixture sit for 30 minutes to allow vegetables to hydrate. Bring mixture back to a boil, then turn down the heat, and cook for 30 minutes or until vegetables are tender. Add water if the soup is thicker than desired.

Place water, oil, and mix in slow cooker. Turn on high for the first 30 minutes. Add additional water if needed, then turn down to low, and simmer until ready to eat.

Italian Navy Bean Soup

Ingredients	6-8 Servings	3-4 Servings	1-2 Servings
Onion	1/4 cup	2 TBS	1 TBS
Celery	4 teaspoons	2 teaspoons	1 teaspoon
Carrots	4 teaspoons	2 teaspoons	1 teaspoon
Garlic	4 teaspoons	2 teaspoons	1 teaspoon
Parsley	4 teaspoons	2 teaspoons	1 teaspoon
Basil	4 teaspoons	2 teaspoons	1 teaspoon
Italian seasoning	4 teaspoons	2 teaspoons	1 teaspoon
TVP ham bits	3/4 cup	6 TBS	3 TBS
Tomato dices	1/4 cup	2 TBS	1 TBS
Tomato powder	1/4 cup	2 TBS	1 TBS
Sugar	2 teaspoons	1 teaspoon	1/2 teaspoon
Spinach	1/4 cup	2 TBS	1 TBS
Navy beans	1 cup	1/2 cup	1/4 cup
Pepper	1/2 teaspoon	1/4 teaspoon	1/8 teaspoon
Salt (optional)	1/2 teaspoon	1/4 teaspoon	1/8 teaspoon
Water	8 cups	4 cups	2 cups
Canola oil	4 teaspoons	2 teaspoons	1 teaspoon

 Heat the water to boiling, remove from heat, add oil, and stir in mix. Cover with a lid, and let the mixture sit for 30 minutes to allow vegetables to hydrate. Bring mixture back to a boil, then turn down the heat, and cook for 30 minutes or until vegetables are tender. Add water if the soup is thicker than desired.

Place water, oil, and mix in slow cooker. Turn on high for the first 30 minutes. Add additional water if needed, then turn down to low, and simmer until ready to eat.

Vegetable Navy Bean Soup

Ingredients	6-8 Servings	3-4 Servings	1-2 Servings
Onion	1/4 cup	2 TBS	1 TBS
Celery	4 teaspoons	2 teaspoons	1 teaspoon
Carrots	4 teaspoons	2 teaspoons	1 teaspoon
Garlic	4 teaspoons	2 teaspoons	1 teaspoon
Parsley	4 teaspoons	2 teaspoons	1 teaspoon
Thyme	1 teaspoon	1/2 teaspoon	1/4 teaspoon
Cloves	1/2 teaspoon	1/4 teaspoon	1/8 teaspoon
TVP ham bits	1 cup	1/2 cup	1/4 cup
Cabbage	4 teaspoons	2 teaspoons	1 teaspoon
Potato dices	1/2 cup	1/4 cup	2 TBS
Navy beans	1 cup	1/2 cup	1/4 cup
Pepper	1/2 teaspoon	1/4 teaspoon	1/8 teaspoon
Salt (optional)	1/2 teaspoon	1/4 teaspoon	1/8 teaspoon
Water	8 cups	4 cups	2 cups
Canola oil	4 teaspoons	2 teaspoons	1 teaspoon

Heat the water to boiling, remove from heat, add oil, and stir in mix. Cover with a lid, and let the mixture sit for 30 minutes to allow vegetables to hydrate. Bring mixture back to a boil, then turn down the heat, and cook for 30 minutes or until vegetables are tender. Add water if the soup is thicker than desired.

Place water, oil, and mix in slow cooker. Turn on high for the first 30 minutes. Add additional water if needed, then turn down to low, and simmer until ready to eat.

Cuban Navy Bean Soup

Ingredients	6-8 Servings	3-4 Servings	1-2 Servings
Onion	1/4 cup	2 TBS	1 TBS
Garlic	2 teaspoons	1 teaspoon	1/2 teaspoon
Carrots	2 teaspoons	1 teaspoon	1/2 teaspoon
Celery	2 teaspoons	1 teaspoon	1/2 teaspoon
Potato dices	4 teaspoons	2 teaspoons	1 teaspoon
Sweet potatoes	4 teaspoons	2 teaspoons	1 teaspoon
Tomato dices	4 teaspoons	2 teaspoons	1 teaspoon
Tomato powder	1/4 cup	2 TBS	1 TBS
Sugar	4 teaspoons	2 teaspoons	1 teaspoon
Cabbage	4 teaspoons	2 teaspoons	1 teaspoon
TVP ham bits	2/3 cup	1/3 cup	8 teaspoons
Navy beans	1 cup	1/2 cup	1/4 cup
Cumin	1/2 teaspoon	1/4 teaspoon	1/8 teaspoon
Parsley	8 teaspoons	4 teaspoons	2 teaspoons
Pepper	1/2 teaspoon	1/4 teaspoon	1/8 teaspoon
Salt (optional)	1/2 teaspoon	1/4 teaspoon	1/8 teaspoon
Water	8 cups	4 cups	2 cups
Canola oil	4 teaspoons	2 teaspoons	1 teaspoon

Heat the water to boiling, remove from heat, add oil, and stir in mix. Cover with a lid, and let the mixture sit for 30 minutes to allow vegetables to hydrate. Bring mixture back to a boil, then turn down the heat, and cook for 30 minutes or until vegetables are tender. Add water if the soup is thicker than desired.

Place water, oil, and mix in slow cooker. Turn on high for the first 30 minutes. Add additional water if needed, then turn down to low, and simmer until ready to eat.

Bean and Ham Soup

Ingredients	6-8 Servings	3-4 Servings	1-2 Servings
Onion	1/4 cup	2 TBS	1 TBS
Garlic	2 teaspoons	1 teaspoon	1/2 teaspoon
Carrots	2 teaspoons	1 teaspoon	1/2 teaspoon
Celery	2 teaspoons	1 teaspoon	1/2 teaspoon
Potato dices	1/4 cup	2 TBS	1 TBS
Sweet potatoes	1/4 cup	2 TBS	1 TBS
Tomato powder	1/4 cup	2 TBS	1 TBS
Sugar	2 teaspoons	1 teaspoon	1/2 teaspoon
Red wine powder	4 teaspoons	2 teaspoons	1 teaspoon
Vinegar powder	4 teaspoons	2 teaspoons	1 teaspoon
TVP ham bits	2/3 cup	1/3 cup	8 teaspoons
Navy beans	1 cup	1/2 cup	1/4 cup
Hickory smoke powder	1/2 teaspoon	1/4 teaspoon	1/8 teaspoon
Red pepper flakes	1/2 teaspoon	1/4 teaspoon	1/8 teaspoon
Pepper	1/2 teaspoon	1/4 teaspoon	1/8 teaspoon
Salt (optional)	1/2 teaspoon	1/4 teaspoon	1/8 teaspoon
Water	8 cups	4 cups	2 cups
Canola oil	4 teaspoons	2 teaspoons	1 teaspoon

Heat the water to boiling, remove from heat, add oil, and stir in mix. Cover with a lid, and let the mixture sit for 30 minutes to allow vegetables to hydrate. Bring mixture back to a boil, then turn down the heat, and cook for 30 minutes or until vegetables are tender. Add water if the soup is thicker than desired.

Place water, oil, and mix in slow cooker. Turn on high for the first 30 minutes. Add additional water if needed, then turn down to low, and simmer until ready to eat.

Navy Bean TVP Ham Chowder

Ingredients	6-8 Servings	3-4 Servings	1-2 Servings
Onion	1/4 cup	2 TBS	1 TBS
Garlic	2 teaspoons	1 teaspoon	1/2 teaspoon
Carrots	2 teaspoons	1 teaspoon	1/2 teaspoon
Celery	2 teaspoons	1 teaspoon	1/2 teaspoon
Sweet potatoes	1/2 cup	1/4 cup	2 TBS
Dry milk	1/3 cup	8 teaspoons	4 teaspoons
TVP ham bits	1 cup	1/2 cup	1/4 cup
Navy beans	1 cup	1/2 cup	1/4 cup
Italian seasoning	2 teaspoons	1 teaspoon	1/2 teaspoon
Pepper	1/2 teaspoon	1/4 teaspoon	1/8 teaspoon
Salt (optional)	1/2 teaspoon	1/4 teaspoon	1/8 teaspoon
Water	8 cups	4 cups	2 cups
Canola oil	4 teaspoons	2 teaspoons	1 teaspoon

Heat the water to boiling, remove from heat, add oil, and stir in mix. Cover with a lid, and let the mixture sit for 30 minutes to allow vegetables to hydrate. Bring mixture back to a boil, then turn down the heat, and cook for 30 minutes or until vegetables are tender. Add water if the soup is thicker than desired.

Place water, oil, and mix in slow cooker. Turn on high for the first 30 minutes. Add additional water if needed, then turn down to low, and simmer until ready to eat.

Smoky Navy Bean Soup

Ingredients	6-8 Servings	3-4 Servings	1-2 Servings
Onion	1/4 cup	2 TBS	1 TBS
Garlic	1 teaspoon	1/2 teaspoon	1/4 teaspoon
Carrots	1 teaspoon	1/2 teaspoon	1/4 teaspoon
Celery	1 teaspoon	1/2 teaspoon	1/4 teaspoon
Potato dices	1/4 cup	2 TBS	1 TBS
Tarragon	1/2 teaspoon	1/4 teaspoon	1/8 teaspoon
TVP ham bits	1 cup	1/2 cup	1/4 cup
Navy beans	1 cup	1/2 cup	1/4 cup
Hickory smoke powder	1 teaspoon	1/2 teaspoon	1/4 teaspoon
Pepper	1/2 teaspoon	1/4 teaspoon	1/8 teaspoon
Salt (optional)	1/2 teaspoon	1/4 teaspoon	1/8 teaspoon
Water	8 cups	4 cups	2 cups
Canola oil	4 teaspoons	2 teaspoons	1 teaspoon

Heat the water to boiling, remove from heat, add oil, and stir in mix. Cover with a lid, and let the mixture sit for 30 minutes to allow vegetables to hydrate. Bring mixture back to a boil, then turn down the heat, and cook for 30 minutes or until vegetables are tender. Add water if the soup is thicker than desired.

Place water, oil, and mix in slow cooker. Turn on high for the first 30 minutes. Add additional water if needed, then turn down to low, and simmer until ready to eat.

Northern Bean Soup Mixes

Northern Beans

All of the soup mixes in this section use northern beans as their primary ingredient. Northern beans, also called great northern beans, are a delicately flavored white bean. They are typically grown in the Midwestern United States, though some people may grow and harvest them elsewhere. Although northern beans are called a white bean, the color is more a cream color.

Northern beans provide many health benefits, having positive effects on:

- lowering cholesterol and triglycerides.
- substantially lowering the risk of type 2 diabetes.
- preventing blood sugar levels from rising too high in people with diabetes.
- providing protection against cancers and heart disease.
- supporting cardiovascular health .
- supporting digestive tract health.
- providing copper and manganese for energy production and antioxidant defense.
- providing folate which helps lower the risk for heart attack, stroke, and peripheral vascular disease.
- increasing energy levels with slow-burning carbohydrates and iron.
- supporting flexibility in blood vessels, bones, and joints.
- maintaining memory with thiamin (vitamin B1).

Northern Beans with Tomato, Onion, and Celery Soup

Ingredients	6-8 Servings	3-4 Servings	1-2 Servings
Northern beans	2 cups	1 cup	1/2 cup
Garlic	4 teaspoons	2 teaspoons	1 teaspoon
Onion	1/4 cup	2 TBS	1 TBS
Celery	1/2 cup	1/4 cup	2 TBS
Tomato dices	1/3 cup	8 teaspoons	4 teaspoons
Tomato powder	1/2 cup	1/4 cup	2 TBS
Sugar	1/4 cup	2 TBS	1 TBS
Parsley	1/4 cup	2 TBS	1 TBS
Beef bouillon	4 teaspoons	2 teaspoons	1 teaspoon
Pepper	1/2 teaspoon	1/4 teaspoon	1/8 teaspoon
Salt (optional)	1/2 teaspoon	1/4 teaspoon	1/8 teaspoon
Water	8 cups	4 cups	2 cups
Olive oil	4 teaspoons	2 teaspoons	1 teaspoon

Heat the water to boiling, remove from heat, add oil, and stir in mix. Cover with a lid, and let the mixture sit for 30 minutes to allow vegetables to hydrate. Bring mixture back to a boil, then turn down the heat, and cook for 30 minutes or until vegetables are tender. Add water if the soup is thicker than desired.

Place water, oil, and mix in slow cooker. Turn on high for the first 30 minutes. Add additional water if needed, then turn down to low, and simmer until ready to eat.

Northern Beans Vegetable Soup

Ingredients	6-8 Servings	3-4 Servings	1-2 Servings
Northern beans	2 cups	1 cup	1/2 cup
Garlic	4 teaspoons	2 teaspoons	1 teaspoon
Onion	1/4 cup	2 TBS	1 TBS
Carrots	1/4 cup	2 TBS	1 TBS
Rosemary	1 teaspoon	1/2 teaspoon	1/4 teaspoon
Parsley	4 teaspoons	2 teaspoons	1 teaspoon
Tomato dices	1/4 cup	2 TBS	1 TBS
Tomato powder	1/4 cup	2 TBS	1 TBS
Sugar	4 teaspoons	2 teaspoons	1 teaspoon
TVP chicken bits	1/4 cup	2 TBS	1 TBS
Chicken bouillon	4 teaspoons	2 teaspoons	1 teaspoon
Pepper	1/2 teaspoon	1/4 teaspoon	1/8 teaspoon
Salt (optional)	1/2 teaspoon	1/4 teaspoon	1/8 teaspoon
Water	8 cups	4 cups	2 cups
Olive oil	4 teaspoons	2 teaspoons	1 teaspoon

Heat the water to boiling, remove from heat, add oil, and stir in mix. Cover with a lid, and let the mixture sit for 30 minutes to allow vegetables to hydrate. Bring mixture back to a boil, then turn down the heat, and cook for 30 minutes or until vegetables are tender. Add water if the soup is thicker than desired.

Place water, oil, and mix in slow cooker. Turn on high for the first 30 minutes. Add additional water if needed, then turn down to low, and simmer until ready to eat.

Garlic Northern Bean Soup

Ingredients	6-8 Servings	3-4 Servings	1-2 Servings
Northern beans	2 cups	1 cup	1/2 cup
Rosemary	2 teaspoons	1 teaspoon	1/2 teaspoon
Thyme	2 teaspoons	1 teaspoon	1/2 teaspoon
Garlic	1/4 cup	2 TBS	1 TBS
Basil	4 teaspoons	2 teaspoons	1 teaspoon
Potato dices	1 cup	1/2 cup	1/4 cup
Onion	4 teaspoons	2 teaspoons	1 teaspoon
Carrots	4 teaspoons	2 teaspoons	1 teaspoon
Parsley	4 teaspoons	2 teaspoons	1 teaspoon
Pepper	1/2 teaspoon	1/4 teaspoon	1/8 teaspoon
Salt (optional)	1/2 teaspoon	1/4 teaspoon	1/8 teaspoon
Water	8 cups	4 cups	2 cups

Heat the water to boiling, remove from heat, and stir in mix. Cover with a lid, and let the mixture sit for 30 minutes to allow vegetables to hydrate. Bring mixture back to a boil, then turn down the heat, and cook for 30 minutes or until vegetables are tender. Add water if the soup is thicker than desired.

Place water and mix in slow cooker. Turn on high for the first 30 minutes. Add additional water if needed, then turn down to low, and simmer until ready to eat.

Pasta Bean Soup

Ingredients	6-8 Servings	3-4 Servings	1-2 Servings
Onion	4 teaspoons	2 teaspoons	1 teaspoon
Garlic	4 teaspoons	2 teaspoons	1 teaspoon
Spinach	1/3 cup	8 teaspoons	4 teaspoons
Butter powder	1/4 cup	2 TBS	1 TBS
Chicken bouillon	4 teaspoons	2 teaspoons	1 teaspoon
Small pasta	1/2 cup	1/4 cup	2 TBS
Northern beans	2 cups	1 cup	1/2 cup
Tomato dices	1/4 cup	2 TBS	1 TBS
Tomato powder	3/4 cup	1/2 cup	1/4 cup
Sugar	4 teaspoons	2 teaspoons	1 teaspoon
Pepper	1/2 teaspoon	1/4 teaspoon	1/8 teaspoon
Salt (optional)	1/2 teaspoon	1/4 teaspoon	1/8 teaspoon
Water	8 cups	4 cups	2 cups
Olive oil	4 teaspoons	2 teaspoons	1 teaspoon
Parmesan cheese	1/4 cup	2 TBS	1 TBS

Heat the water to boiling, remove from heat, add oil, and stir in mix. Cover with a lid, and let the mixture sit for 30 minutes to allow vegetables to hydrate. Bring mixture back to a boil, then turn down the heat, and cook for 30 minutes or until vegetables are tender. Add water if the soup is thicker than desired. Top with parmesan cheese.

Place water, oil, and mix in slow cooker. Turn on high for the first 30 minutes. Add additional water if needed, then turn down to low, and simmer until ready to eat. Top with Parmesan cheese before serving.

Pinto Bean
Soup Mixes

Pinto Beans

The soup mixes in this section have pinto beans as their primary ingredient. Pinto beans have a beige background strewn with reddish brown splashes of color. They are like little painted canvases, hence their name "pinto," which in Spanish means "painted." When cooked, their colored splotches disappear, and they become a beautiful pink color.

Pinto beans provide many health benefits, having positive effects on:

- lowering cholesterol and triglycerides.
- substantially lowering the risk of type 2 diabetes.
- preventing blood sugar levels from rising too high in people with diabetes.
- supporting cardiovascular health.
- supporting digestive tract health.
- providing copper and manganese for energy production and antioxidant defense.
- providing folate which helps lower the risk for heart attack, stroke, and peripheral vascular disease.
- increasing energy levels with slow-burning carbohydrates and iron.
- maintaining memory with thiamin (vitamin B1).

Southwestern Pinto Bean Soup

Ingredients	6-8 Servings	3-4 Servings	1-2 Servings
Garlic	1 1/2 teaspoon	3/4 teaspoon	1/2 teaspoon
Onion	1/4 cup	2 TBS	1 TBS
Cumin	1 teaspoon	1/2 teaspoon	1/4 teaspoon
Cayenne pepper	1/2 teaspoon	1/4 teaspoon	1/8 teaspoon
TVP chicken bits	3/4 cup	6 TBS	3 TBS
Tomato dices	1/2 cup	1/4 cup	2 TBS
Tomato powder	1/4 cup	2 TBS	1 TBS
Sugar	2 teaspoons	1 teaspoon	1/2 teaspoon
Chicken bouillon	2 teaspoons	1 teaspoon	1 teaspoon
Cilantro	1 teaspoon	1/2 teaspoon	1/4 teaspoon
Chives	1 teaspoon	1/2 teaspoon	1/4 teaspoon
Pinto Beans	1 cup	1/2 cup	1/4 cup
White cheese powder	1/4 cup	2 TBS	1 TBS
Pepper	1/2 teaspoon	1/4 teaspoon	1/8 teaspoon
Salt (optional)	1/2 teaspoon	1/4 teaspoon	1/8 teaspoon
Water	8 cups	4 cups	2 cups
Canola oil	4 teaspoons	2 teaspoons	1 teaspoon

Heat the water to boiling, remove from heat, add oil, and stir in mix. Cover with a lid, and let the mixture sit for 30 minutes to allow vegetables to hydrate. Bring mixture back to a boil, then turn down the heat, and cook for 30 minutes or until vegetables are tender. Add water if the soup is thicker than desired.

Place water, oil, and mix in slow cooker. Turn on high for the first 30 minutes. Add additional water if needed, then turn down to low, and simmer until ready to eat.

TVP Ham Pinto Bean Soup

Ingredients	6-8 Servings	3-4 Servings	1-2 Servings
Onion	1/4 cup	2 TBS	1 TBS
Celery	2 teaspoons	1 teaspoon	1/2 teaspoon
Garlic powder	2 teaspoons	1 teaspoon	1/2 teaspoon
TVP ham bits	3/4 cup	6 TBS	3 TBS
Marjoram	1/2 teaspoon	1/4 teaspoon	1/8 teaspoon
Thyme	1/2 teaspoon	1/4 teaspoon	1/8 teaspoon
Pinto beans	2 cups	1 cup	1/2 cup
Pepper	1/2 teaspoon	1/4 teaspoon	1/8 teaspoon
Salt (optional)	1/2 teaspoon	1/4 teaspoon	1/8 teaspoon
Water	8 cups	4 cups	2 cups
Canola oil	4 teaspoons	2 teaspoons	1 teaspoon

Heat the water to boiling, remove from heat, add oil, and stir in mix. Cover with a lid, and let the mixture sit for 30 minutes to allow vegetables to hydrate. Bring mixture back to a boil, then turn down the heat, and cook for 30 minutes or until vegetables are tender. Add water if the soup is thicker than desired.

Place water, oil, and mix in slow cooker. Turn on high for the first 30 minutes. Add additional water if needed, then turn down to low, and simmer until ready to eat.

Pinto Bean Soup

Ingredients	6-8 Servings	3-4 Servings	1-2 Servings
Onion	1/4 cup	2 TBS	1 TBS
Garlic	1 teaspoon	1/2 teaspoon	1/4 teaspoon
TVP ham bits	1 cup	1/2 cup	1/4 cup
Pinto beans	1 cup	1/2 cup	1/4 cup
Red pepper flakes	1/4 teaspoon	1/8 teaspoon	1 dash
Pepper	1/2 teaspoon	1/4 teaspoon	1/8 teaspoon
Salt (optional)	1/2 teaspoon	1/4 teaspoon	1/8 teaspoon
Water	8 cups	4 cups	2 cups
Canola oil	4 teaspoons	2 teaspoons	1 teaspoon

Heat the water to boiling, remove from heat, add oil, and stir in mix. Cover with a lid, and let the mixture sit for 30 minutes to allow vegetables to hydrate. Bring mixture back to a boil, then turn down the heat, and cook for 30 minutes or until vegetables are tender. Add water if the soup is thicker than desired.

Place water, oil, and mix in slow cooker. Turn on high for the first 30 minutes. Add additional water if needed, then turn down to low, and simmer until ready to eat.

Split Pea Soup Mixes

Split Peas

The soup mixes in this section contain split peas as a primary ingredient. Split peas originated from the field pea that was native to central Asia and Europe. Dried split peas have been consumed since prehistoric times with fossilized remains being found at archeological sites in Swiss lake villages.

Peas are mentioned in the Bible and were prized by the ancient civilizations of Egypt, Greece, and Rome. Peas were introduced into the United States soon after the colonists first settled here. Today the largest commercial producers of dried peas are Russia, France, China, and Denmark. Once they are dried and the skins removed, they split naturally.

Split peas provide many health benefits, having positive effects on:

- lowering cholesterol and triglycerides.
- substantially lowering the risk of type 2 diabetes.
- preventing blood sugar levels from rising too high in people with diabetes.
- reducing risk of certain health conditions, including breast and prostate cancer.
- supporting cardiovascular health.
- supporting digestive tract health.
- providing copper and manganese for energy production and antioxidant defense.
- providing folate which helps lower the risk for heart attack, stroke, and peripheral vascular disease.
- increasing energy levels with slow-burning carbohydrates and iron.
- maintaining memory with thiamin (vitamin B1).

TVP Ham Split Pea Soup

Ingredients	6-8 Servings	3-4 Servings	1-2 Servings
Onion	4 TBS	2 TBS	1 TBS
Carrots	4 teaspoons	2 teaspoons	1 teaspoon
Celery	4 teaspoons	2 teaspoons	1 teaspoon
Potato dices	1/2 cup	1/4 cup	2 TBS
Chicken bouillon	4 teaspoons	2 teaspoons	1 teaspoon
Marjoram	1 teaspoon	1/2 teaspoon	1/4 teaspoon
Poultry seasoning	1 teaspoon	1/2 teaspoon	1/4 teaspoon
Sage	1 teaspoon	1/2 teaspoon	1/4 teaspoon
Basil	4 teaspoons	2 teaspoons	1 teaspoon
Split peas	2 cups	1 cup	1/2 cup
TVP ham bits	1/2 cup	1/4 cup	2 TBS
Pepper	1/2 teaspoon	1/4 teaspoon	1/8 teaspoon
Salt (optional)	1/2 teaspoon	1/4 teaspoon	1/8 teaspoon
Water	8 cups	4 cups	2 cups
Olive oil	4 teaspoons	2 teaspoons	1 teaspoon

Heat the water to boiling, remove from heat, add oil, and stir in mix. Cover with a lid, and let the mixture sit for 30 minutes to allow vegetables to hydrate. Bring mixture back to a boil, then turn down the heat, and cook for 30 minutes or until vegetables are tender. Add water if the soup is thicker than desired.

Place water, oil, and mix in slow cooker. Turn on high for the first 30 minutes. Add additional water if needed, then turn down to low, and simmer until ready to eat.

Savory Split Pea Soup

Ingredients	6-8 Servings	3-4 Servings	1-2 Servings
Onion	1/4 cup	2 TBS	1 TBS
Carrots	4 teaspoons	2 teaspoons	1 teaspoon
Celery	4 teaspoons	2 teaspoons	1 teaspoon
Potato dices	4 teaspoons	2 teaspoons	1 teaspoon
Parsley	4 teaspoons	2 teaspoons	1 teaspoon
Cloves	1/2 teaspoon	1/4 teaspoon	1/8 teaspoon
Split peas	2 cups	1 cup	1/2 cup
TVP ham bits	1/2 cup	1/4 cup	2 TBS
Pepper	1 teaspoon	1/2 teaspoon	1/4 teaspoon
Salt (optional)	1/2 teaspoon	1/4 teaspoon	1/8 teaspoon
Water	8 cups	4 cups	2 cups
Olive oil	4 teaspoons	2 teaspoons	1 teaspoon

Heat the water to boiling, remove from heat, add oil, and stir in mix. Cover with a lid, and let the mixture sit for 30 minutes to allow vegetables to hydrate. Bring mixture back to a boil, then turn down the heat, and cook for 30 minutes or until vegetables are tender. Add water if the soup is thicker than desired.

Place water, oil, and mix in slow cooker. Turn on high for the first 30 minutes. Add additional water if needed, then turn down to low, and simmer until ready to eat.

Buttery Split Pea Soup

Ingredients	6-8 Servings	3-4 Servings	1-2 Servings
Onion	1/4 cup	2 TBS	1 TBS
Leeks	4 teaspoons	2 teaspoons	1 teaspoon
Celery	4 teaspoons	2 teaspoons	1 teaspoon
Butter powder	1/2 cup	1/4 cup	2 TBS
Tomato dices	4 teaspoons	2 teaspoons	1 teaspoon
Tomato powder	4 TBS	2 TBS	1 TBS
Sugar	2 teaspoons	1 teaspoon	1/2 teaspoon
Split peas	2 cups	1 cup	1/2 cup
Lentils	4 TBS	2 TBS	1 TBS
Pepper	1/2 teaspoon	1/4 teaspoon	1/8 teaspoon
Salt (optional)	1/2 teaspoon	1/4 teaspoon	1/8 teaspoon
Water	8 cups	4 cups	2 cups
Olive oil	4 teaspoons	2 teaspoons	1 teaspoon

 Heat the water to boiling, remove from heat, add oil, and stir in mix. Cover with a lid, and let the mixture sit for 30 minutes to allow vegetables to hydrate. Bring mixture back to a boil, then turn down the heat, and cook for 30 minutes or until vegetables are tender. Add water if the soup is thicker than desired.

Place water, oil, and mix in slow cooker. Turn on high for the first 30 minutes. Add additional water if needed, then turn down to low, and simmer until ready to eat.

Old-Timer's Split Pea Soup

Ingredients	6-8 Servings	3-4 Servings	1-2 Servings
Onion	1/4 cup	2 TBS	1 TBS
Carrots	4 teaspoons	2 teaspoons	1 teaspoon
Celery	4 teaspoons	2 teaspoons	1 teaspoon
Beef bouillon	4 teaspoons	2 teaspoons	1 teaspoon
Thyme	1/8 teaspoon	1/8 teaspoon	1/8 teaspoon
Split peas	2 cups	1 cup	1/2 cup
TVP ham bits	1 cup	1/2 cup	1/4 cup
Pepper	1 teaspoon	1/2 teaspoon	1/4 teaspoon
Salt (optional)	1/2 teaspoon	1/4 teaspoon	1/8 teaspoon
Water	8 cups	4 cups	2 cups
Canola oil	4 teaspoons	2 teaspoons	1 teaspoon

Heat the water to boiling, remove from heat, add oil, and stir in mix. Cover with a lid, and let the mixture sit for 30 minutes to allow vegetables to hydrate. Bring mixture back to a boil, then turn down the heat, and cook for 30 minutes or until vegetables are tender. Add water if the soup is thicker than desired.

Place water, oil, and mix in slow cooker. Turn on high for the first 30 minutes. Add additional water if needed, then turn down to low, and simmer until ready to eat.

Curry Split Pea Soup

Ingredients	6-8 Servings	3-4 Servings	1-2 Servings
Onion	1/4 cup	2 TBS	1 TBS
Carrots	4 teaspoons	2 teaspoons	1 teaspoon
Celery	4 teaspoons	2 teaspoons	1 teaspoon
Curry powder	4 teaspoons	2 teaspoons	1 teaspoon
Split peas	2 cups	1 cup	1/2 cup
TVP ham bits	1 cup	1/2 cup	1/4 cup
Pepper	1 teaspoon	1/2 teaspoon	1/4 teaspoon
Salt (optional)	1/2 teaspoon	1/4 teaspoon	1/8 teaspoon
Water	8 cups	4 cups	2 cups
Olive oil	4 teaspoons	2 teaspoons	1 teaspoon

 Heat the water to boiling, remove from heat, add oil, and stir in mix. Cover with a lid, and let the mixture sit for 30 minutes to allow vegetables to hydrate. Bring mixture back to a boil, then turn down the heat, and cook for 30 minutes or until vegetables are tender. Add water if the soup is thicker than desired.

Place water, oil, and mix in slow cooker. Turn on high for the first 30 minutes. Add additional water if needed, then turn down to low, and simmer until ready to eat.

Resources

There are many resources that sell dehydrated vegetables,
fruits, spices, and cooking products. The resources listed
below are some of my favorite vendors.

Harmony House Foods
www.harmonyhousefoods.com
Telephone: (800) 696-1395

The Grain mill of Wake Forest
www.thegrainmillwf.com
Telephone: (919) 526-4573

Spices etc
www.spicesetc.com
Telephone: (800) 827-6373

The Great American Spice Co
www.americanspice.com
Telephone: (260) 420-0500

Amazon
www.amazon.com

Ingredient to Recipe Index

Ingredient to Recipe Index cont'd.

Ingredient to Recipe Index cont'd.

Ingredient to Recipe Index cont'd.

Ingredient to Recipe Index cont'd.

Ingredient to Recipe Index cont'd.

Ingredient to Recipe Index cont'd.

CPSIA information can be obtained at www.ICGtesting.com
Printed in the USA
BVOW022312170313

315601BV00004B/10/P